Reading CAE

Eight practice tests for the
Cambridge C1 Advanced

Jane Turner

PROSPERITY EDUCATION

PROSPERITY EDUCATION
www.prosperityeducation.net

Registered offices: Sherlock Close, Cambridge
CB3 0HP, United Kingdom

© Prosperity Education Ltd. 2021

First published 2021

ISBN: 978-1-913825-28-7

For further information and resources, visit:
www.prosperityeducation.net

To infinity and beyond.

Contents

Introduction

Welcome to this edition of sample tests for the Cambridge C1 Advanced, Reading (Parts 5–8).

This resource comprises eight whole Reading tests, detailed answer keys and write-in answer sheets.

Author **Jane Turner** is an ELT materials writer and consultant who is currently based in Cambridge, UK. She holds an MA in Education Management and Cambridge DELTA, and is an associate lecturer in EAP/EFL at Anglia Ruskin University.

The content has been written to closely replicate the Cambridge exam experience, and has undergone comprehensive review. You or your students, if you are a teacher, will hopefully enjoy the wide range of essay topics and benefit from the repetitive practice, something that is key to preparing for this part of the C1 Advanced (CAE) examination.

For me, having prepared many students for this and other Cambridge exams, pre- and post-2015, when the specification changed, it is Paper 1 that poses the biggest challenge. Without there being much support available by way of quality practice material, students struggle to gain the necessary levels of confidence in the Reading and Use of English section prior to sitting the exam. Therefore, in my classes, after studying and working through the core knowledge required, we drill, drill and drill exercises in preparation for the exams.

I hope that you will find this resource a useful study aid, and I wish you all the best in preparing for the exam.

Michael Macdonald
Madrid, 2021

Other titles for the C1 Advanced

Visit www.prosperityeducation.net to view our wide range of Cambridge exam-practice resources (B2–C2).

Use of English
Ten practice tests for the
Cambridge C1 Advanced

Michael Macdonald

CAE Parts 1–4

2018

978-1795776141

100 pages

Use of English
Ten more practice tests for the
Cambridge C1 Advanced

Billie Jago

CAE Parts 1–4

2020

978-1916129771

100 pages

English Master
C1 Key Word Transformation
200 exercises

Margaret Cooze

FCE Part 4

2020

978-1916129757

100 pages

Forthcoming 2021:

Speaking CAE by Luis Porras Wadley

www.prosperityeducation.net

Cambridge C1 Advanced Reading: Parts 5–8

Test 1

You are going to read an introduction to a book in which the writer discusses a radio programme. For questions 31–36, mark the appropriate answer (A, B, C or D) that you think fits best according to the text.

Introduction to a book about the BBC Shipping Forecast

A well-worn cliché about the British is that they are a 'proud seafaring nation'. One popular argument that seemingly supports this is the abundance of English idioms that derive from life on the open seas. However, whether this is convincing evidence of a continued bond with the sea is debatable. Phrases like 'cut and run' and 'learning the ropes' are so ingrained in modern usage that most people are probably ignorant of their roots. Those interested in Britain's relationship with the sea should explore other aspects of popular culture for valuable insights.

Top of this list may well be the national shipping forecast, of all things. Advising listeners of storm warnings and providing detailed weather reports of the coastal waters surrounding the UK, this meteorological report has been broadcast over the radio waves for more than one hundred and fifty years. It clearly performs a vital function for the relatively small proportion of the population that can make sense of the specialist terminology used in the broadcast, and who rely on it to protect them. Yet, curiously, the expressions used in these bulletins appear on commercial products, including posters, cups and t-shirts, and have even found their way into song lyrics by some of the UK's most famous bands. The popularity of the programme now extends far beyond its intended audience, reaching those for whom it serves no obvious practical purpose.

That this broadcast is held in such high regard may seem absurd. Nevertheless, interest in the programme is undeniable. Public outcry and political debate have followed attempts to introduce even minor changes to the programme's format. Understanding the shipping forecast as a cultural phenomenon has been a source of interest for many researchers. Scholars have drawn on a diverse range of academic disciplines, including sociology, media studies and psychology, to shed light on the mainstream appeal of such a specialist programme. Undoubtedly, there is much to be gained from this multidisciplinary approach. However, most research remains focused on the narrow theme of the sea and sailing. These works portray the shipping forecast as the cultural embodiment of the nation's innate affinity for anything maritime.

What follows from this is that most scholarly work on the shipping forecast largely prioritises the concept of heritage. The main argument is that listeners tune in for a fond reminder of past times. Given that the UK's ship-building traditions also attract media attention and even tourism revenue, this argument may seem at least partially attractive. Furthermore, some schools continue to teach naval history as part of the curriculum. It may well be that, for at least some shipping forecast fans, having background historical knowledge enhances listeners' appreciation of the programme. However, this does not entirely explain why the shipping forecast resonates with as many people as it does. After all, unfamiliarity with British history is by no means an obstacle to enjoying the shipping forecast. If it were, why then does the programme attract global audiences?

Thus, this book explores alternative interpretations. Of course, one must never lose sight of the fact that, first and foremost, the programme's main function is to *inform*. Nevertheless, the way the specialist data are presented in the shipping forecast is unlike any other weather report. Its unique sentence patterns and rhythms are both difficult to understand yet at the same time soothing. With this in mind, I explore in this book the poetic qualities of the shipping forecast. Expanding on articles I have previously published on the therapeutic qualities of oral communication, I argue that poetry is the key to understanding the shipping forecast's appeal. It is surely no coincidence that many listeners tucked up in their beds rely on the calm and gentle rhythm of the bulletins to help them sleep at night.

Another assumption is challenged in this book, namely that the shipping forecast is an entirely British invention. It developed from its nineteenth-century origins thanks, in no small part, to pioneering navigational work by an American sailor. This, in combination with an international agreement signed in Brussels in 1853, enabled important shipping data to be shared. But far from spoiling its alluring sense of mystery, I hope that uncovering the truth will strengthen readers' appreciation for this wonderful programme.

31 In the first paragraph, what point does the writer make about English idioms related to the sea?

    A The prevalence of these expressions is a unique feature of English.

    B The original meanings of these expressions should be highlighted.

    C The cultural significance of these expressions can be challenged.

    D The popularity of these expressions is impossible to measure.

32 What do the words 'their way' refer to in line 13?

    A goods purchased by the general public

    B experts studying weather in coastal areas

    C linguistic terms in the shipping forecast

    D radio programmes about meteorology

33 What does the writer suggest about the shipping forecast in the third paragraph?

    A Public affection for it has been underestimated.

    B It has been exploited for political purposes.

    C Attempts to analyse it require knowledge of different subjects.

    D Academic research conducted on it tends to be limited in scope.

34 The writer says that analysing the shipping forecast from a historical perspective:

    A results in an incomplete understanding of the programme's appeal

    B reduces the pleasure listeners get from the programme

    C helps us understand why the programme attracts diverse audiences

    D highlights the academic value of studying the programme.

35 The writer refers to poetry in the fifth paragraph to show that:

    A artistic and scientific fields can support each other

    B it is possible to appreciate something without fully understanding it

    C linguistic structure can have a powerful impact on people

    D the spoken word is the most effective way to communicate complex ideas.

36 The text suggests that the main aim of the book is to:

    A investigate social attitudes to the shipping forecast

    B question popular beliefs about the shipping forecast

    C argue for the educational importance of the shipping forecast

    D celebrate lesser-known aspects of the shipping forecast.

You are going to read four reviews of a book about the role of entrepreneurs in society. For questions 37–40, select the correct review (A–D) using the separate answer sheet. The reviews may be selected more than once.

Movers and Money Makers, by Joy Anwari

Reviewer A

Having drawn on her experiences as a former business owner to illustrate complex sociological ideas in previous works, it was only a matter of time before renowned sociologist and broadcaster Joy Anwari would write a book about entrepreneurship. In *Movers and Money Makers*, Anwari explores the status of entrepreneurs in contemporary society. For better or worse, the nation's leading entrepreneurs have become recognisable media figures. They are routinely consulted on matters of government policy, and some of them have played important roles in educational initiatives. More generally, Anwari asserts that becoming an entrepreneur has gained aspirational status in the last few decades. With the references to popular culture and broadcast media that have become her hallmark, Anwari provides compelling evidence for the growing social influence of entrepreneurs. Frustratingly, what remains unanswered in *Movers and Money Makers* is whether such power is ultimately for the benefit or to the detriment of society. Despite this, *Movers and Money Makers* offers a fascinating insight into modern business.

Reviewer B

Publishing extensively on subjects such as the rituals of domestic life, the hidden purposes of small talk, and changing social norms regarding marriage, Professor Joy Anwari has a well-deserved reputation as a sociologist who marries intellectual thought with the ability to communicate her ideas with clarity. This is in evidence again in *Movers and Money Makers,* which focuses on the world of business. Anwari uses a wide variety of examples that successfully demonstrate how the profile of entrepreneurs has risen in recent times. Such an argument is difficult to deny in an age in which successful business leaders often become household names. However, set against the high standard of Anwari's previous publications, *Movers and Money Makers* misses the mark somewhat. Where is the willingness to challenge mainstream assumptions or present ideas that may feel uncomfortable to the reader? It's tempting to conclude that Anwari's own links to the business world prevent her from being more objective in this instance.

Reviewer C

Start-ups have gone mainstream. So claims academic Joy Anwari in *Movers and Money Makers.* Anwari herself once ran a successful media firm before swapping boardrooms for lecture halls. While this lends a degree of personal authority to the book, *Movers and Money Makers* is in no way a 'how-to' guide for would-be entrepreneurs. Instead, Anwari attempts to shed light on the burgeoning socio-cultural status of modern-day entrepreneurs. For instance, Anwari discusses the role of entrepreneurs as drivers of social change. She is unquestionably adept at conveying theoretical concepts to non-experts. However, her arguments are flawed or unconvincing at times, most notably because she fails to draw a clear distinction between the corporate world in general and entrepreneurs in particular. Even so, readers who have enjoyed Anwari's previous works will find this book equally as entertaining.

Reviewer D

Are the nation's business leaders role models for society, and if so, shouldn't they be subject to closer scrutiny for their actions? Curiously, Joy Anwari demonstrates uncharacteristic reluctance to delve into such discussions in her latest book, *Movers and Money Makers*. In a departure from the commentary found in her other titles, *Movers and Money Makers* makes little attempt to suggest the wider implications of the central theme. A missed opportunity, despite the book's undeniable quality. We are taken on a thrilling historical journey that charts the changing fortunes of entrepreneurs in society. Anwari persuades us that today's business leaders hold positions of influence quite unlike anything their historical counterparts would have experienced. To do this, she draws from literature, legislation and journalism, and the depth of her research is certainly impressive. Anwari's enthusiastic prose will no doubt appeal to readers, even though they may be left questioning the ultimate purpose of the book.

Which reviewer:

expresses a similar concern to Reviewer A about the scope of the book?	**37**
has a different opinion from the others about how effectively Anwari defends the main point in her book?	**38**
has a different opinion to Reviewer C about how Anwari's professional credentials affect the content of the book?	**39**
has a similar view to Reviewer B that *Movers and Money Makers* is unlike Anwari's other books?	**40**

You are going to read an extract from a magazine article. Six paragraphs have been removed. Select from the paragraphs (A–G) the one that fits each gap (41–46). There is one extra paragraph that you do not need to use.

Seed Banking

The world's book repositories, university libraries and manuscript archives are surely the ultimate cultural treasure trove. From obscure scientific texts to landmark literary works, via long-forgotten political treatises and correspondence between historical figures, these institutions preserve all the published output ever produced. Archivists and librarians use innovative technology and traditional techniques to protect ancient works from the ravages of time. These custodians of the written word are committed to the safeguarding of our shared cultural and social history for future generations.

41

This is no minor undertaking. The storage vaults used by seed banks to house their collections are designed to withstand extreme weather conditions and other external threats. The administrators of seed banks also make every effort to optimise conditions within their facilities to conserve their vast array of diverse and often ancient plant species. Humidity and temperature levels are scrupulously regulated, enabling even ancient seeds to be stored. In so doing, the seeds are primed for future use, should the need arise.

42

Thinking along these lines seems only prudent given the significant consequences of climate change. As global temperatures rise and pollution levels increase, it's vital that we consider the fate of the planet's vegetation and, by extension, the wildlife it supports. Seed banks enable us to preserve vital crops that would otherwise be at risk of extinction. Likewise, seed banks can mitigate the harm caused by flooding, droughts or forest fires. Such measures may safeguard species that are rare or of special scientific interest, not to mention crops used in agriculture.

43

While some seed banks are intended to be repositories or stores of seeds that can be used in order to replenish stocks, others take a more 'productivist' approach. Some seed banks engage in genetic modification and cross-breeding programmes, enabling agri-businesses to develop new plant species designed to optimise crop yields.

44

Ethical concerns aside, the inherent efficacy of seed banking has been challenged. Some studies have suggested that 36% of the world's plant species at critical risk of extinction produce recalcitrant seeds. In lay terms, many plant species simply cannot tolerate the scientific processes involved in seed banking, namely the drying and freezing of seeds. The quality of these seeds would degrade to such an extent that seed banking simply wouldn't be a viable option.

45

Assuming that seed banks are even able to ascertain which seeds to store, and that these species can survive the seed-banking process, there remains the question of *ex situ* conservation. Many specimens end up in collections in which the plants are not endemic or would not normally flourish. Even if the captive plant species can adapt to new locations, doing so would be at the genetic expense of their ability to survive in their native environment. For this reason, conservationists argue that attempting to preserve species at their source would be a preferable approach.

46

A Viewed from this perspective, a seed bank is arguably more akin to that of a financial institution than that of a cultural organisation. Seed banking is an environmental insurance policy designed to keep our world as ecologically rich and biologically diverse as possible, like 'saving for a rainy day'.

B Interestingly, this highlights yet another parallel to be drawn between seed banks and cultural institutions, such as libraries and museums. Any endeavour intended to benefit society may need to come under the auspices of public ownership.

C Another perceived shortcoming is the complexity involved in identifying which seeds should be banked. It is not always easy to predict which seed varieties will be of the greatest use to humankind in the future, or indeed how long the seeds can be stored without any form of degradation.

D Fortunately, however, recent cutting-edge innovations such as cryopreservation offer promising, albeit costly, on-site ways to preserve an even greater variety of species than seed banking alone can. When used in conjunction with seed banking, there is hope for the future of the planet's bio-diversity.

E As well as lessening the potentially harmful impact of natural disasters on plant life, seed banks can make another significant ecological contribution. The specimens stored in these banks can also be utilised for research purposes, helping scientists discover more about the genetic variation of different plant species.

F Seed banks display comparable dedication to their mission. Storing the seeds of the world's plants and trees, these banks do far more than merely cataloguing ancient botanical species out of intellectual curiosity. They are guardians of bio-diversity and food security by ensuring supplies of viable seeds for cultivation in the future.

G However, this brave new world of scientific innovation is not without criticism. Some commentators are concerned about large corporations wielding their power to patent new plant varieties, or, at the very least, the genetic codes for these seeds. This raises fundamental questions regarding the ownership and control of seeds, and how it could potentially exacerbate economic disparity.

You are going to read a magazine article in which five sports industry experts share their views on esports. For questions 47–56, select the expert (A–E) using the separate answer sheet. The experts may be selected more than once.

Which expert makes the following statements?

It is difficult to identify an aspect of mainstream sport that is missing from esports.	**47**
People's participation in esports has no bearing on their interest in other activities.	**48**
Esports can be used as an additional activity to help people improve certain physical skills.	**49**
Many of the skills that team games teach can also be developed via gaming.	**50**
Fitness is a must for gamers involved at the highest level of esports.	**51**
Audiences are unlikely to be impressed by esports events.	**52**
There is substantial demand for broadcasters to pay attention to esports events.	**53**
The gaming community may suffer if its tournaments are integrated into other sporting events.	**54**
There is scope for esports to increase in popularity.	**55**
The controversial content of some video games is detrimental to esports' reputation.	**56**

Esports

Should esports be treated as an athletic endeavour? We've asked five sports experts to share their views on this increasingly popular pastime.

Expert A

The rising popularity of esports has confounded industry experts who predicted it would be a passing fad. Ordinarily, such cynicism would be understandable. It is notoriously difficult to identify which trends will capture the public's imagination. Yet esports has enjoyed an ardent and engaged following right from the outset, arguably setting it apart from other trends that have emerged in recent years. Therefore, sponsors and broadcasters should have recognised esports' untapped potential far sooner. Instead, rather than mainstream media outlets raising the profile of esports and thereby broadening its appeal, they are now scrambling to capitalise on fans' thirst for esports coverage. The same goes for the corporate world, with companies now eager to be aligned with gaming tournaments. There's no reason why esports can't extend its reach even further in the future.

Expert B

The prospect of gaming appearing at the Olympic Games would be highly contentious, and ultimately wouldn't serve esports well. Not only would it fail to inspire spectators expecting to watch exceptional athletic feats, it could potentially alienate the existing esports fan base if it were overshadowed by more famous sports. Professional gamers, no doubt, train incredibly hard and are of course gifted, but similar levels of dedication and technical skill are required for countless activities that wouldn't be classified as sports. If esports deserves a place at the Olympics, what about chess? An ever-changing roster of events has featured in the Olympic programme in recent years, but in the quest to broaden its remit, the Olympic movement must still adhere to the fundamentals of what actually constitutes sport.

Expert C

There have always been people whose definition of sport encompasses only a very narrow range of traditional athletic pursuits. However, the case of gaming highlights how arbitrary the label 'athlete' can be. Quite apart from the hours of training, strategic coaching and mental concentration involved in reaching the elite level of competition, esports professionals are also expected to be in peak physical condition.

Physical conditioning has both direct and indirect performance benefits in esports. Not only can it improve players' motor skills, but it also helps players develop the stamina to perform throughout their long, intense competitions. And just like professional athletes in many conventional sporting disciplines, sports psychology is now a routine part of the esports training regimen. How, then, does an esports professional differ from an Olympic athlete?

Expert D

The popularity of esports doesn't necessarily mean that young people have swapped their running shoes for games consoles. Enjoyment of gaming doesn't preclude youngsters from taking up other sports, even if, in reality, gaming and traditional sports generally attract different audiences. In fact, in the case of children for whom team sports are unappealing, gaming can be an effective way for them to acquire the skills they would ordinarily learn through playing sport with their peers. Indeed, esports is a worthwhile pursuit for all children. Studies have shown that young people can derive as many social and intellectual benefits from esports as they can from other leisure activities, including team sports. If esports is opening up opportunities for more children to benefit from team activities, then that is to be applauded.

Expert E

Anecdotal evidence suggests that mastering certain esports can actually help athletes enhance their abilities in areas such as fine motor skills, hand-eye coordination and response times. In fact, gaming has become a popular activity amongst professional athletes in a variety of sports. It's clear that gaming and traditional sports aren't mutually exclusive, but, even so, the recognition or promotion of esports by official sporting bodies remains problematic. Sports associations, especially those with a global audience, have to exercise extreme caution when endorsing esports. After all, many esports tournaments are based around games that appear to glorify violence. Of course, there are countless exceptions to this, but unless and until esports moves more in line with the wholesome image of professional sport, gaming will always be difficult to market as a mainstream proposition.

Name _____   Date _____

Part 5

Mark the appropriate answer (A, B, C or D).

0	A	B	C	D

31	A	B	C	D		34	A	B	C	D
32	A	B	C	D		35	A	B	C	D
33	A	B	C	D		36	A	B	C	D

Part 6

Add the appropriate answer (A–D).

37	38	39	40

Part 7

Add the appropriate answer (A–G).

41	42	43
44	45	46

Part 8

Add the appropriate answer (A–E).

47	48	49	50	51
52	53	54	55	56

Cambridge C1 Advanced
Reading: Parts 5–8

Test 2

You are going to read a review of a book about sports. For questions 31–36, mark the appropriate answer (A, B, C or D) that you think fits best according to the text.

Onside, by Miriam Carter

Whenever someone discovers that I mainly write about the leisure industry, they invariably recount some version of the following quip: 'Well, it's easy to know when someone does hot yoga, because they'll immediately tell you all about it.' Any initial amusement I may have got from this joke soon faded with every re-telling, regardless of whether the hobby in question was fell running, open-water swimming or fly fishing. As the punchline implies, devotees of some pastimes seemingly attach unusually great importance to advertising their commitment to their chosen hobby. Curiously, they appear to derive more validation from other people's perceptions of their leisure habits than from any intrinsic joy that comes from actually doing the activity. But is it truly the case that certain pursuits carry more social value than others, and is that why people feel the need to boast about them?

Miriam Carter explores such matters in her latest book, *Onside*. The opening chapter focuses on the apparent connection between leisure activity and status, and proposes that choice of leisure pursuit reveals much about a person's standing in society. For instance, since some hobbies entail exotic foreign trips or prohibitively expensive equipment, choice of leisure pursuit is obviously, to an extent, related to one's economic means. But as Carter points out, this alone cannot explain why some activities gain mass appeal while others retain a limited following. Thus, *Onside* examines the historical factors underpinning why some activities, described as 'prestige signifiers', remain the preserve of the elite in society, while others attract different groups, or are universally enjoyed.

Making no concession to cultural relativism, *Onside* depicts social attitudes to leisure as universal, rather than context-specific. This is undoubtedly a premise that can be challenged. After all, winter sports such as skiing may be viewed as elitist pastimes in some societies, yet so commonplace in others that they confer no particular social currency at all. Nevertheless, Carter's discussion of class connotations certainly reinforces the point that numerous factors influence how we choose to spend our free time.

Another thread running throughout *Onside* is that of self-image. Carter suggests that hobbies can be an effective means by which we can cultivate and present a particular brand to the world. The implication is that certain social values or character traits have become associated with specific pastimes and, by extension, the people who do them. So far, so uncontroversial. Yet, while it's hardly a stretch to imagine that physically demanding pursuits such as marathon running are more likely to appeal to people who are naturally determined or goal-oriented, the book raises more illuminating points on how the role of leisure has changed in contemporary society. For instance, access to hitherto niche or 'minority' sports has widened in recent years, with people trying activities that they may never have considered in the past. Carter explores this phenomenon by drawing a link between the issue of self-image and what she refers to as 'leisure tribalism'. This concept is one of the core themes of the book.

In *Onside*, 'tribalism' denotes a sense of inclusion or belonging that, according to Carter, is becoming an increasingly important influence. Carter argues that there has been a shift in people's relationship with their hobbies in recent years, with people now expecting far more than simple enjoyment. Apparently, people strive to find activities which can become an integral part of their identity. Put simply, it is no longer enough to take up running. Instead, one must *be* a runner and, ideally, part of a specific running 'tribe'. Though contentious, it's a point that resonates, at least partially. As a recent convert to powerlifting, I can vouch for the powerful feeling of acceptance I gained from being welcomed into powerlifting communities, both real and virtual. Whether I now feel defined by my hobby is a matter of debate.

Onside consolidates Miriam Carter's reputation as an engaging writer. She aims to offer fresh perspectives on familiar topics, and she achieves this by combining academic rigour and entertaining prose. However, the arguments in *Onside* rarely veer beyond the obvious, despite the impressive range of complex theories and obscure case studies cited. Ultimately, one wonders whether Carter's fondness for intellectualising the banal has reached its limits.

31 In the first paragraph, what point does the reviewer make about people's attitudes to leisure?

    A Expressing enthusiasm for leisure is viewed as a negative in some societies.

    B Discussing leisure habits is a source of personal pride for many people.

    C Certain pastimes are more likely to attract ridicule from other people.

    D People take their free-time pursuits more seriously nowadays.

32 What do the words 'this alone' refer to in line 14?

    A financial considerations

    B choice of hobby

    C one's social status

    D travelling for leisure purposes

33 In the third paragraph, the reviewer says that the book:

    A lacks detail in its coverage of the influence of class on leisure trends

    B relies too much on analysing different cultural interpretations of leisure

    C misrepresents how some leisure pursuits are perceived by different social groups

    D ignores the importance of context when examining perceptions of leisure.

34 The reviewer refers to marathon running as an example of an activity that:

    A transcends limitations of social class

    B attracts a specific type of personality

    C has grown in popularity in recent times

    D develops participants' ability to focus.

35 According to the fifth paragraph, what point does the book make about tribalism?

    A It has changed what people hope to gain from their hobbies.

    B It has made people more open to finding new leisure activities.

    C It has enhanced the enjoyment many people get from their hobbies.

    D It has strengthened the bonds between people with shared interests.

36 What does the reviewer suggest about Miriam Carter's writing?

    A Her selection of evidence is questionable.

    B Her simple writing style is effective.

    C She focuses too much on academic analysis.

    D She challenges popular assumptions.

You are going to read four extracts from articles in which academics discuss environmentalism. For questions 37–40, choose from the academics A–D. The academics may be selected more than once. Mark your answers on the separate answer sheet.

Environmentalism in Society

Academic A

The use of social media platforms to disseminate information about nature conservation is often cited as evidence that society is becoming more conscious of environmental issues. The claim that never before has there been such public engagement in green matters may seem tempting, but I would dispute the notion that environmentalism has finally achieved mass appeal in society. Rather, social media has facilitated the sharing of information between like-minded individuals. Social media campaigns are merely updated versions of the types of work undertaken by environmental activists in the second half of the twentieth century. Without a doubt, digital innovation has helped environmentalists spread their message, but let's not overstate its ability to set the green agenda. For evidence of a fundamental shift in environmental thinking, we must look to legislation and political cooperation between states as the true barometer of society's progress.

Academic B

Environmentalists are justifiably concerned about corporate 'greenwashing'. The general consensus is that while many companies are keen to be associated with environmental principles, this has yielded little quantifiable action. The claims made by companies about the ecological credentials of their products or production processes are dubious at best, and, potentially, intentionally misleading. Nevertheless, there has been a shift in the public's expectation of companies, and consequently there is increasing demand for corporate transparency and accountability. This heightened scrutiny may be forcing companies to reconsider their actions. In any case, evidence is emerging that, whatever the source of their motives, positive steps are in fact being taken by companies in the sphere of sustainability. Clearly, more research should be conducted to measure the long-term impact of such measures, but I do believe that progress is being made. There are causes for cautious optimism, even if we are wise to remain sceptical.

Academic C

That expressions like 'sustainability' and 'eco-friendly' have entered common linguistic usage underlines how environmentalism has moved into the mainstream, to the extent that one might even question whether the movement's core principles have been corrupted or at least diluted. Vigilance is required to ensure that commercial motives do not undermine the objectives of those striving for a more equitable deal for the planet. Even so, there has been a genuine shift in society's attitudes to environmental issues. When it comes to public policy, no longer are concerns about the environment seen as niche or subordinate to issues such as healthcare, education or the economy. Indeed, the greatest successes in the green movement have been achieved by demonstrating that environmental sustainability is an integral aspect of economic and social development. Governments now realise that it falls to them to take greater environmental responsibility. Without this vital step, nothing meaningful can be achieved.

Academic D

Expressing interest in environmental protection is hardly a contentious viewpoint in contemporary society. Indeed, opposition to it now generates significantly more controversy. From an academic perspective, it has been fascinating to observe how environmentalism has transcended its origins as an alternative movement challenging social norms. It's surely no coincidence that public interest in environmental issues has grown as the world has become increasingly connected. The ease with which individuals across the globe can now connect and share their experiences has played a major role in normalising and popularising the subject of environmental sustainability. The growing influence of online activism has been particularly notable in terms of raising public awareness of corporate accountability. Even so, protecting the environment has unfortunately yet to become a core feature of corporate practice. It is worth emphasising that corporate engagement in environmental issues rarely moves beyond being a supplementary activity primarily intended for marketing purposes.

Which academic:

expresses a different view to Academic D regarding the impact of companies' efforts to protect the environment?	**37**
expresses a different view to Academic A about the influence of technology on public attitudes to the environment?	**38**
agrees with Academic D concerning changes in public perceptions of environmental issues?	**39**
expresses a similar view to Academic C about which stakeholder in society has the ultimate responsibility for environmental change?	**40**

You are going to read an extract from a magazine article. Six paragraphs have been removed. Select from the paragraphs (A–G) the one that fits each gap (41–46). There is one extra paragraph that you do not need to use.

Having a laugh?

Mika Sommers explores laughter yoga

The best piece of advice I ever received as an aspiring journalist was to develop an open mind. What I didn't realise at that time was that open-mindedness was one of the key skills required of you should you ever find yourself as a features writer for a lifestyle magazine one day!

41	

That wasn't the only reservation I had. I've always enjoyed having a good giggle with friends as a form of social stress relief. Even so, it took all my professional training as an open-minded journalist to embrace the prospect of spending an entire day laughing awkwardly with complete strangers.

42	

The point of difference is of course in its use of laughter as a therapeutic tool. Since the human body cannot differentiate between simulated laughter and the real thing, practitioners claim we can train ourselves to harness the positive effects of laughter whenever we want. We can apparently access the feel-good chemicals produced when we laugh, regardless of how we're actually feeling at the time. Moreover, pretending to laugh is believed to create genuine joy in itself.

43	

Making it work in practice is an entirely different matter. In the workshop, we repeatedly vocalised the sounds and rhythms of different types of laughter, from quiet sniggers, to the roaring laughter we might make when encountering something hilarious. This felt extremely embarrassing at first, promoting me to conclude that laughter yoga simply wasn't for me.

44	

Devotees argue that this sense of teamwork is another feature that makes laughter yoga unique. During the workshop, we did whatever suggestions our groupmates offered, such as pretending to be trains or animals. Working with different partners made it feel like a safe environment in which we could be silly without judgement.

45	

Interestingly, the physical effects of laughter yoga are well-documented in scientific literature. When performed correctly and safely, the combination of stretches, deep-laughter drills and breathing exercises can have a profound effect on muscles. Laughter yoga has even been described as 'internal jogging'. That's why it attracts a committed following around the world, and is far from being a passing fad.

46	

A If nothing else, my experience did force me out of my comfort zone. I wouldn't necessarily sign up for a full course, but I have incorporated some of the principles into my daily life. Above all, it's made me feel less concerned about making a fool of myself in social situations, something that has helped me overcome both personal and professional obstacles. Being open-minded does indeed pay off.

B This is the first myth that laughter yoga practitioners are keen to dispel. It turns out that the sessions don't revolve around spontaneous, uncontrollable laughter. Instead, a considerable portion of the time is spent on simple stretching and breathing exercises. If the aim of laughter yoga were simply to reduce stress through physical relaxation, there would be little to distinguish it from numerous other well-being trends.

C I'm glad that I persevered with the workshop despite my initial lack of ability. The exercises are designed to challenge you and the tutors help you make sense of the complicated moves. I hadn't realised that laughing involved so much physical exertion, but by the end of the session, I was able to get more out of the tasks.

D Fortunately, it didn't take long for my initial discomfort to fade. Soon, the awkward, self-conscious laughter inexplicably turned to genuine glee. All my fellow participants were exchanging looks as if none of us could quite believe what we were doing. Before long, we were encouraging one another to go further, be even sillier, laugh even louder. It felt very liberating!

E Having left the workshop feeling relaxed, and invigorated, I had to admit that laughter yoga was more enjoyable than I'd expected it to be. Another benefit emerged the following day. What I hadn't fully appreciated at the time was just how strenuously your body is working during the session. I was amazed to discover that my entire body ached as if I'd been lifting weights.

F Interestingly, the 'fake it until you make it' approach is commonplace in many fields, perhaps most notably in sport. Sport psychologists encourage athletes to visualise themselves becoming world champions, as this can have a discernible impact on their performance. Laughing oneself happy is essentially an extension of this.

G Regular readers of this column will know that I'm often required to report on some rather bizarre lifestyle trends. None more so than my latest assignment, in which I found myself pondering the correct attire for a whole-day 'laughter yoga' workshop. Should my outfit be funny to make other people laugh, or comfortable to enable me to perform complicated yoga poses?

You are going to read a magazine article in which five experts share their views about the role of drama in education. For questions 47–56, select the expert (A–E) using the separate answer sheet. The experts may be selected more than once.

Which expert makes the following statements?

External influences can determine how schools organise their timetables.	47
Do not confuse drama as a specialist subject with drama as a class activity.	48
Drama can be particularly useful when teaching career-based skills.	49
Drama lessons are an important way to expose students to culture.	50
Educational experts are becoming increasingly in favour of teaching drama.	51
Drama deserves a place on the school curriculum.	52
More needs to be done to improve the quality of drama teaching in schools.	53
Drama should be offered to all pupils, regardless of their level of talent.	54
Drama can enhance learners' experience of many different subjects.	55
There is a need for additional study on some aspects of drama teaching.	56

Should drama take centre stage?

Do students benefit from studying drama? We've asked five experts to share their views on incorporating drama into education.

Expert A

Discussion about the role of drama in education has always focused on whether drama should be taught as a mandatory subject. Educationists, policy-makers and of course other interested stakeholders may raise a raft of pertinent points supporting or opposing this proposition, but that shouldn't preclude drama from featuring in other lessons. At its core, drama teaches students a range of communicative and interpersonal skills that are easily transferable to other school subjects and beyond. For instance, role-play dialogues, arguably the most accessible of drama activities, can be used to great effect in other subjects, including foreign languages, literature and even history. We must ensure that any debates about the place of drama lessons in the school timetable are kept distinct from the use of drama activities as a valid pedagogical tool.

Expert B

Creative subjects such as drama continue to attract substantial attention from educational experts. However, most of the research has been directed towards the implications for schools and colleges, and whether these subjects can achieve positive learning outcomes for students. Conversely, relatively little research has been conducted in the area of drama teaching in higher education contexts. Further light should be shone on this area because universities are becoming increasingly creative with their teaching techniques and their use of drama. Many such institutions are discovering that drama is an ideal means by which students can gain meaningful practical experience in areas related to their future careers. For instance, common drama activities, like improvisation exercises, can help medical students learn more about interacting with anxious patients.

Expert C

While the benefits of exposing students to the arts are generally accepted, there has been a shift in recent years away from focusing on performance-related disciplines. Inevitably, given the increasing governmental scrutiny schools are under regarding students' performance in formal exams, some establishments are reluctant to allocate teaching time to those subjects that are not formally assessed. Instead, priority is given to what are considered core subjects, such as maths and science, to appease education authorities. Overlooking subjects like drama in this way is incredibly short-sighted and misguided. However, attitudes to education and teaching approaches tend to go in cycles. Hopefully, drama and other arts subjects will be reinstated and be taught at school again before long.

Expert D

Performing arts are well established in many educational contexts around the world, but the approaches taken to the teaching of drama vary. In some countries, drama is treated as a niche subject that should only be offered to students displaying an innate aptitude for creative subjects. These students are encouraged to pursue drama and it is even presented as a viable career path. What this approach fails to recognise is that drama has intrinsic value in itself, regardless of a student's future aspirations or natural ability. It enriches students' lives by helping them discover new worlds of possibility. Restricting some students' access to drama, or indeed any creative subject, simply because they are deemed to lack certain skills is wrong. Not only will it reinforce the idea that the arts are elitist, but it could also prevent students from broadening their creative horizons.

Expert E

It's encouraging to see that the teaching of drama now receives widespread support within most educational circles. This certainly hasn't always been the case, but the consensus now seems to be that drama shouldn't be regarded as an optional extra. This represents a fundamental shift from traditional, assessment-focused views of education towards a more holistic approach in which learners' individual strengths, needs and interests should be considered. However, in the rush to incorporate drama teaching into the school curriculum, we must ensure that it is done to the same rigorous standards as with any other subject. Unless drama classes are taught by specialist teachers with professional training, the concern is that drama will continue to be on the periphery, rather than an integral part of the school experience.

Name _____

Date _____

Part 5

Mark the appropriate answer (A, B, C or D).

0	A	B	C	D

31	A	B	C	D		34	A	B	C	D
32	A	B	C	D		35	A	B	C	D
33	A	B	C	D		36	A	B	C	D

Part 6

Add the appropriate answer (A–D).

37	38	39	40

Part 7

Add the appropriate answer (A–G).

41	42	43
44	45	46

Part 8

Add the appropriate answer (A–E).

47	48	49	50	51
52	53	54	55	56

PROSPERITY EDUCATION
www.prosperityeducation.net

Cambridge C1 Advanced
Reading: Parts 5–8

Test 3

You are going to read an introduction to a book about linguistics. For questions 31–36, mark the appropriate answer (A, B, C or D) that you think fits best according to the text.

Language Matters

Like all the best unsolved mysteries, the complexities of language are a source of fascination for many people, whether academic experts or interested lay persons. Take childhood linguistic development, for instance. For decades, competing theories have sought to identify the processes involved in the journey from unintelligible babbling to linguistically complex, meaningful sentences. Consensus has yet to be reached on this intriguing aspect of human development. Nevertheless, since the 1950s, there has been a notable shift away from the once dominant behaviourist model of language acquisition. In fact, the term 'acquisition' itself reflects the modern view that children do something other than merely mimic whatever linguistic stimuli they encounter. Of course, this may come as a surprise to any parent driven to distraction by their toddler repeating every single thing they hear. Regardless, current thinking on the subject now presents language as an instinctive tendency rather than as a skill to be practised and perfected through trial and error.

While *Language Matters* summarises the key theoretical principles of these behaviorist and innatist models of language development, the focus of this book is largely practical. After all, the language-acquisition process is more likely to be comprehended when applied in real-life contexts. And as an educator, I make no apologies for doing so from the perspective of language instruction. Thus, my intention is to highlight the extent to which language acquisition theories have informed both previous and current language-teaching practice, especially within the school environment. Readers are invited to draw their own conclusions about the effectiveness of these practices, based on their own personal experiences. For instance, anyone who has ever been forced to memorise disconnected lists of vocabulary or endure endless 'listen–repeat' language drills may wish to consider what theoretical foundation such activities are based on, or indeed, what practical purpose they actually serve.

Perhaps the more pressing question is whether people still want to study a foreign language at all. There is genuine concern about the shrinking profile of foreign-language learning in education, evidenced by the dwindling uptake of language degrees. Likewise, many schools are axing or significantly reducing their language provision. As with most matters of education policy, a combination of 'push' and 'pull' factors are probably involved in this. For instance, a decline in the number of qualified language teachers and the growing importance of technology-based subjects, such as ICT, could both feasibly play a role. What's more, any resultant lack of exposure to languages at school will naturally affect students' access to university language programmes. Fortunately, language learning is actually enjoying quite a revival outside of formal educational contexts. There has never been a better time to learn a language, given all the digital tools currently at our disposal. Demand for language-learning apps, websites, social media groups and online courses is booming, underlining our continued enthusiasm for languages.

Language forms an integral part of the human experience. We can be moved to tears by poetry or feel utterly baffled by the grammatical rules of an unfamiliar language. How many of us have been persuaded to part with our cash after hearing a persuasive sales pitch, or inspired to vote for a particular candidate on the basis of their powerful rhetoric? Language can be the source of great national pride, too. Tales about the supposed origins of unique expressions or even regional accents in our native language get passed down and, over time, enter folklore. It's clear, then, that we feel strongly attached to language, which is why any perceived changes to our own language can result in fierce debate.

Every so often, a prominent educator alleges that language standards have slipped. The argument is typically that today's youth are ignorant of 'correct' language usage and the baffling new expressions they coin are a sign of how society has been 'corrupted' by everything from technology to foreign TV shows. The implication is that schools must do more to curb these tendencies. Yet, as *Language Matters* explores, language has never been set in stone. Rather, language is fluid and alive. Linguistic conventions change over time, usually as a reflection of changes in society. That we can re-shape language to express ourselves with clarity and precision should be celebrated.

31 In the first paragraph, the writer suggests that contemporary theories of language development:

    A pay less attention to the idea of conscious learning

    B focus too much on the importance of the external environment

    C are increasingly influenced by behaviourist perspectives

    D acknowledge the importance of both capability and repetition.

32 What do the words 'doing so' refer to in line 15?

    A understanding theories

    B teaching languages

    C applying concepts

    D explaining principles

33 What does the author imply about the language-teaching activities mentioned in the second paragraph?

    A Learners find them boring.

    B They are likely to produce positive outcomes.

    C They are growing in popularity.

    D Teachers use them for many different reasons.

34 In the third paragraph, the writer draws a distinction between:

    A teachers' and students' attitudes to learning a foreign language

    B the popularity of language learning within education and society in general

    C the positive and negative factors affecting language education policy

    D language-teaching approaches within school and online settings.

35 In the fourth paragraph, the writer refers to popular stories to:

    A question the importance of grammatical rules

    B demonstrate the impact of language on our emotions

    C suggest that languages evolve over time

    D highlight the relationship between culture and language.

36 In the fifth paragraph, what point does the writer make about language?

    A The creativity of language is often ignored by educators.

    B Society has historically been shaped through language.

    C Language can be regarded as having elastic properties.

    D Language should be protected from harmful influences.

You are going to read four reviews about a documentary on social media influencers. For questions 37–40, choose from the reviewers A–D. The reviewers may be selected more than once. Mark your answers on the separate answer sheet.

Influencers and Icons

Four reviewers comment on Andi Fuyako's latest documentary

Reviewer A

In *Influencers and Icons*, Andi Fuyako explores the considerable pressures many social media personalities face. These influencers, especially those who have built their entire careers around projecting a particular image, are expected to be both charmingly authentic yet constantly alert to every single thing they say, do, and post. While it may be hard for us to have total sympathy for them, Fuyako successfully conveys the downside to this increasingly aspirational career. Having to present a carefully curated version of reality at all times must eventually take its toll, no matter how great the financial incentives. In this refreshingly honest documentary, the viewer is shown the reality: we see that influencers' enjoyment of life has been replaced with persistent agonising over how their actions will be perceived by their followers. It is both infuriating and baffling. *Influencers and Icons* is less a commentary about the relentless rise of social media influencers, and more a critique on the pursuit of fame.

Reviewer B

Despite being billed as a fly-on-the-wall documentary, *Influencers and Icons* may leave the viewer curious about how authentic the scenes actually were. The parts where influencers complain about all the sacrifices they have to make for their chosen career seem particularly far-fetched. Whether these scenes were somewhat manipulated for dramatic purposes only Andi Fuyako will know, but they do prove that, behind all the glamour and excitement of being an online influencer, a lot of hard work is involved. Of course, most influencers' support comes mainly from the notoriously fickle youth sector, so, unless they continually keep up with the latest trends, many online personalities find that their influence is short-lived. In fact, and as we see in the documentary, these people spend hours perfecting their SEO rankings and algorithms, and devising commercially shrewd plans to stay ahead of their rivals. This may dispel the popular notion that these influencers are talentless, but is this the best use of their skills?

Reviewer C

Perhaps the most controversial social media influencers are the so-called 'lifestyle gurus'. These people, who often lack even basic accreditation or professional credentials, post endlessly about all manner of dubious diet and nutrition fads. Unfortunately, many of their fans don't realise that this content is nothing more than advertising, and that the products in question may in fact be ineffective at best or even potentially harmful. Why, then, does Andi Fuyako barely cover this issue in *Influencers and Icons*? In a documentary following genuine influencers, not once are these people challenged about this, or whether they ever stop to consider the consequences of their content. This would have made for a far more illuminating documentary, especially since *Influencers and Icons* features several lifestyle influencers with first-hand experience of promoting dietary supplements and 'energy drinks'. What is the point of a real-life documentary if it doesn't reveal the issues that matter?

Reviewer D

No matter how slick the production values of a TV or magazine campaign may appear to traditional audiences, conventional advertising isn't particularly effective at reaching the much-coveted teen markets. Instead, social media celebrities – so-called influencers – are becoming increasingly vital because they have instant access to millions of impressionable youngsters. As *Influencers and Icons* reveals, the top influencers can earn substantial amounts from corporate sponsors by promoting particular products online. Fuyako's entertaining documentary follows influencers with differing levels of fame, but the core theme throughout is the extent to which companies now influence these people's online content. More should have been made of the ethical questions this raises, and this, I feel, is to the detriment of the documentary. Even so, it was fascinating to discover how often these influencers rely on marketing strategy and business acumen in their work. I applaud Fuyako for providing a real glimpse into their strange online world.

Which reviewer:

has a different opinion to Reviewer D regarding the main aim of the documentary?	**37**

expresses a similar view to Reviewer D concerning influencers' key abilities?	**38**

has a different opinion to the others about whether the documentary was realistic?	**39**

has a similar opinion to Reviewer C about a shortcoming of the documentary?	**40**

You are going to read an extract from a magazine article. Six paragraphs have been removed. Select from the paragraphs A–G the one that fits each gap (41–46). There is one extra paragraph that you do not need to use.

Taking the plunge

Paul Harris explores the wild swimming phenomenon

Swimming can be an effective form of exercise, but it isn't always an enjoyable experience. If you associate swimming with doing monotonous laps in an over-chlorinated pool while dodging the arms and legs of overtaking swimmers, then it won't necessarily be a pastime that fills you with joy. However, swimming in a lake or river is an entirely different proposition to splashing about in a municipal pool, and one that may well convince you of the benefits of exercising in water.

| 41 | |

Of course, people have been swimming outside for centuries, long before swimming pools were built. Perhaps the current craze for wild swimming represents a nostalgic yearning to recreate childhood memories of care-free days spent by the river. Yet, there are also plenty of individuals taking it up for the first time, which would explain the steep rise in internet searches for basic information about wild swimming. Whether it is a renewed interest or a brand-new hobby, it is predominantly city dwellers driving this trend.

| 42 | |

With that in mind, the growing profile of wild swimming may simply be an extension of a more general appreciation of the benefits of nature. The psychological benefits of being in nature have been well documented, and fans of wild swimming often extol the restorative qualities of a quick dip in a cold lake. Likewise, 'forest bathing' is another nature-based practice to have gained prominence in recent years, and involves relaxation techniques harnessing the sensory benefits of trees.

| 43 | |

An enticing prospect perhaps, but one that is not without its risks. Swimming in an unfamiliar body of water requires constant alertness to one's surroundings, especially when in unpredictable or fast-moving currents. Novices are strongly advised to swim with more experienced individuals, at least until they become more confident. Those new to wild swimming should also remember that, depending on location, water temperatures can range from refreshingly cool to ice cold. While this is certainly invigorating, it is important for the body to acclimatise.

| 44 | |

This point is surely underlined by the fact that wild swimming has found a following amongst serious athletes of many different disciplines. Some athletes do it for strength or endurance conditioning to supplement their existing regime. Others, especially those competing in water-based events, might incorporate wild swimming into their training in order to focus on specific elements of their technique, such as stroke length, breathing patterns or pacing. The added physical challenges of swimming in nature add dimensions that swimming in a pool cannot replicate.

| 45 | |

From the relaxing to the taxing, it is clear that outdoor swimming is a pastime that can be enjoyed on many different levels. The proliferation of official bodies and associations promoting it can only serve to raise its profile further, and it is encouraging to note that these organisations prioritise the safety of participants at all times. However, it is also imperative that outdoor swimmers make every effort to respect the environment while they venture out into streams, rivers and lakes.

| 46 | |

A Undoubtedly, prolonged periods in urban environments can have a significant toll on people, so perhaps the growing appeal of wild swimming for urbanites is more about the setting than the activity itself. After all, there are few opportunities to reconnect with nature in the concrete jungle.

B In fact, the very notion that it is now known as 'wild swimming', or 'open water swimming', may be rather telling of its growing interest within metropolitan circles. For people living in rural areas, where it is common practice to take advantage of lakes and streams, it is simply 'swimming'.

C In fact, the energy expenditure involved in keeping warm is just one of the reasons why wild swimming is often significantly more gruelling than swimming in a pool. When you also factor in the strength required to keep afloat in rough water, the physical benefits are indisputable.

D Actually, a dislike of pool-based swimming isn't necessary to appreciate the joys of wild swimming. Happy groups of swimming enthusiasts are an increasingly common sight in our rivers, lakes and ponds. Clubs seeking beautiful spots to swim are popping up across the nation.

E This responsibility doesn't lie solely with swimmers. Local and national initiatives play a pivotal role in keeping waterways clean and pollution-free, and safeguarding aquatic ecology. As wild swimmers will no doubt agree, take care of nature and nature will take care of you.

F However, one key difference between wild swimming and activities based around mindfulness in nature is, of course, the inherent physical challenge it involves. Some wild swimmers maintain that it is precisely this sense of pushing one's limits that they relish.

G As well as providing physical-conditioning options for sporting professionals, open-water swimming is a thrilling competitive discipline in its own right. Gruelling open-water swimming races, either as part of triathlons or as separate events, are now attracting mainstream audiences.

You are going to read a magazine article in which five commentators discuss space exploration. For questions 47–56, select the commentator (A–E) using the separate answer sheet. The commentators may be selected more than once.

Which commentator makes the following statements?

Space research policy should not be informed by public opinion.	47
Most of the work done by space programmes does not receive the recognition it deserves.	48
The success of space programmes is difficult to quantify.	49
Too much importance is attached to economic factors when planning space projects.	50
Breakthroughs in technology are often the result of support from the private sector.	51
Policy makers are increasingly conscious of public opinion when making budgetary decisions.	52
Some of the benefits created by space exploration are long-term propositions.	53
It is difficult to overlook the environmental damage that space exploration causes.	54
Business opportunities in space are, to a certain extent, limited by financial considerations.	55
There is scope for space exploration to involve both commercial and scientific purposes.	56

Space Exploration

What is to be gained from space research? We've asked five experts to share their views on the implications of space exploration.

Commentator A

Concerns about the growing role that private companies are playing in space exploration are misguided. In reality, the corporate world has always been at the forefront of scientific innovation. Most of the technology we rely on in our daily lives would never have been developed in the first place without an economic impetus driving innovation. I see no reason why private companies should not invest in space programmes, assuming that this does not lead to a conflict of ethical interest on the part of scientists, or interferes with the mission of the programmes. Nevertheless, the International Space Station is an important symbol of how nations can and should cooperate for the benefit of scientific endeavour and, ultimately, humanity. The work conducted there should take precedence over projects commissioned by commercial enterprises.

Commentator B

Space research is often sensationalised by the media for the sake of dramatic headlines. Frustratingly, this leads to inaccurate reporting about serious academic research. While the media is preoccupied with the existence of alien life, mundane (but far more vital) research that forms the main body of work in space is ignored. The vast majority of research conducted on the International Space Station has direct implications for our planet, like the search for mineral resources, or atmospheric research. There is a danger that media circulation of myths and half-truths could sway public opinion against space exploration altogether. In the current climate, in which governments have to account for every single public expenditure, politicians are incredibly sensitive to any claims that they are wasting public money. If funding for essential scientific research is put in jeopardy as a result of such apparent waste, the whole world would suffer.

Commentator C

Intellectual curiosity spurs scientists to push the boundaries of human knowledge, which is to be applauded. From an academic viewpoint, the milestones reached over the past two decades in the field of space exploration are incredible and justifiably celebrated. Yet, for every achievement, there is also a compromise to be made. Regarding space exploration, there is always an environmental price to be paid. While missions into space expand our knowledge about threats to our planet, they also actively contribute to environmental problems here on Earth, mainly through their vast consumption of fossil fuels. Whether this is a price worth paying for the advancement of scientific knowledge is hard to know, but unless these missions can reduce their emissions, enthusiasm for them will decline.

Commentator D

Public interest in space exploration is heartening to see, and it is right that space programmes that involve public funding come under close scrutiny. Providing that it doesn't determine or alter the decisions space agencies take while planning their programmes, public debate of and engagement in scientific matters should in fact be encouraged. The real issue we are facing now is that, when the financial stakes are so high, this interferes with the aims of space programmes. This unfortunately puts significant constraints on the types of research space agencies can conduct, especially when the most worthwhile projects cannot be evaluated in terms of simple, measurable outcomes. While corporate sponsorship is touted as a viable alternative to government funding, this will inevitably harm the integrity of space programmes. Science should not be at the mercy of market forces.

Commentator E

Space travel is generally discussed in relation to its scientific possibilities, but increasingly, there are economic opportunities to be explored. For instance, commercial space tourism is still in its infancy, but there is undeniable interest in it despite the prohibitively high costs involved. As the technology develops, it will gradually become more affordable and, therefore, a viable option for a greater proportion of people. However, investors hoping to make immediate profits from space travel are advised to consider alternative ventures. A more lucrative option in the immediate term is in the removal of 'space junk'. Incredibly, space exploration causes vast amounts of debris, in the form of satellites that have fallen out of orbit and detritus from space vehicles. As this problem becomes increasingly pressing, demand for enterprising firms that can resolve this issue is growing.

Name _____

Date _____

Part 5

Mark the appropriate answer (A, B, C or D).

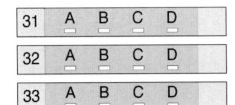

Part 6

Add the appropriate answer (A–D).

37 | 38 | 39 | 40

Part 7

Add the appropriate answer (A–G).

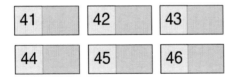

Part 8

Add the appropriate answer (A–E).

47 | 48 | 49 | 50 | 51
52 | 53 | 54 | 55 | 56

Cambridge C1 Advanced
Reading: Parts 5–8

Test 4

You are going to read an introduction to a magazine article about the antiques trade. For questions 31–36, mark the appropriate answer (A, B, C or D) that you think fits best according to the text.

Antiques and Culture

Forget trendy cafes or cool art galleries; for me the hallmark of any truly decent city is an abundance of excellent antique shops. It's certainly something I love about my city. There, many antique shops are located in the upmarket areas, although I personally prefer those in the more low-key neighbourhoods. I genuinely believe that, whether they sell objects that are rare and expensive, or charmingly unremarkable, antique shops offer us a more intimate and accessible glimpse into the past than museums can. Bustling vintage markets shouldn't be overlooked either, particular if you're easily seduced by quirky items, as many younger customers are. To my mind though, nothing can beat a *proper* antique shop where you can browse in peace, and where the knowledgeable staff will gladly tell you about the fascinating origins of the items, and guide you if you need help. It's such an enjoyable, hassle-free way to spend an afternoon.

Aside from antique shopping as a leisure activity, the lure of the objects themselves is undeniable. Naturally, aesthetic styles go in and out of fashion, but the quality of antiques has never been in doubt. There is simply no comparison between hand-crafted antique furniture, which was built to last, and flimsy, mass-produced modern equivalents. Similarly, people are becoming increasingly conscious of the environmental choices they make as consumers, and are moving away from cheap, disposable products that wreak significant damage on our planet. This, more than anything, explains the current boom in antique sales. Then again, antiques have always had a broad appeal, a point reflected in the fact that TV shows about antiques are rating hits among viewers of all ages. Perhaps we are naturally drawn by the intrigue of objects from bygone times.

Talking of intrigue, the mysterious business of identifying an antique remains a fascinating philosophical puzzle to me. Many people will only regard certain, specific decorative items, or pieces of furniture, as antiques. Yet, if functional items like chairs or bookcases can be classed as antiques, what about golf clubs or musical instruments? Should an object's appearance or its purpose take precedence over the item's age in this classification? 'Contemporary' inevitably becomes 'vintage' over time, but grandparents, children, archaeologists, interior designers and historians would surely measure this using different timescales. In commercial terms, it used to be the case that only objects over a hundred years old were classified as antiques. However, this rule is no longer strictly applied. To complicate matters further, nowadays some businesses even refer to 'modern antiques', which sounds like a contradiction in terms.

Perhaps the term 'modern antiques' acknowledges that most buyers prioritise items that fit in with their lifestyles. For instance, demand for the heavy and large, ornate furniture of the nineteenth century has declined in recent years. Sadly, as beautiful and well-made as they are, items from this period are simply impractical in modern homes where space can be extremely limited. However, it is encouraging to see that there has been a surge in sales of sleek, streamlined 'mid-century' pieces from the 1950 and 1960s. This particular period is characterised by its use of materials that were considered cutting-edge at the time but which we now take for granted. From a design point of view, incorporating these pieces into a modern home still adds a sense of history, but the overall effect is harmonious rather than jarring.

The antiques industry moves with the times and is not averse to innovation. For instance, online traders – in some cases extremely large ones – have now entered the market, offering alternative ways to buy and sell antiques. In many instances, this is intended to supplement the firm's existing product offerings. Even if this doesn't match my idealised image of knowledgeable, specialist antique shops, there is logic in the move. After all, it gives consumers the opportunity to compare brand-new products alongside their vintage counterparts.

As someone with a keen interest in antiques, I'm relieved that there is still an obvious, general affection for objects from the past, whether these be centuries-old oak cabinets or futuristic-looking lamps from the 1960s. It's heartening to see the sector flourishing in cosy shops, thriving vintage markets and via online antiques retailers. Ultimately, antiques encourage people to consume in a more responsible, low-waste way. Appreciating our past may well help to safeguard our future.

31 In the first paragraph, the writer suggests they are mainly attracted to antique shops because they:

    A sell products which reflect their location

    B help preserve historical traditions

    C offer items that are unique

    D provide a pleasant customer experience.

32 According to the second paragraph, what is the main reason for the popularity of antiques nowadays?

    A The ecological benefits of antique products.

    B Renewed interest in vintage design styles.

    C The superior quality of antique products.

    D Increased media coverage of antiques.

33 In the third paragraph, what point does the writer make about the classification of antiques?

    A The age of an antique can be interpreted in multiple ways.

    B The term 'antique' may be used to mislead customers.

    C What constitutes an antique is surprisingly difficult to define.

    D Both form and function are considered when evaluating antiques.

34 What is implied about nineteenth-century furniture in the fourth paragraph?

    A It is more attractive than antique pieces from other periods.

    B Customers are wrong to overlook this type of furniture.

    C The design of this furniture is too plain for current tastes.

    D This type of furniture looks strange in modern interiors.

35 What does the word 'it' refer to in line 42?

    A using the internet to buy antiques

    B adding antique items to a company's business

    C focusing specifically on antique products

    D trading in the antiques market

36 What is the aim of the article?

    A To promote interest in buying antiques.

    B To explain how the antiques trade has developed.

    C To express concern for the antiques retail sector.

    D To evaluate different types of antiques trade.

You are going to read four reviews of a book about historical figures. For questions 37–40, choose from the reviewers A–D. The reviewers may be selected more than once. Mark your answers on the separate answer sheet.

Learning from History
Four reviewers comment on Louis Black's new book

Reviewer A

The old adage that history is 'written by the victors' suggests that there is only one possible reading of history: an interpretation based solely on the perspective of those on the 'winning' side of events. In reality, of course, interpretations of history are far from fixed, a point reinforced in Louis Black's fast-paced new book, *Learning from History*. In it, Black seeks to highlight how our views of history have evolved. Thus, *Learning from History* is a historical overview of historical analyses. The decision to focus on individual figures rather than the events themselves is a curious one, but it certainly suits Black's lively narrative style. What could have been rather a dull work in the hands of less engaging writers is brought to life thanks to Black's ability to add intrigue even to well-known historical figures. *Learning from History* will, no doubt, satisfy Black's loyal following of history buffs, while possibly even converting a few others.

Reviewer B

Learning from History by Louis Black profiles a varied range of the most notable, or at least notorious, figures from world history. Indeed, the geographical scope of the book deserves praise, as Black sheds light on key figures from regions often overlooked in history courses. Black's gossipy tone throughout is irresistibly entertaining, too. His portrayal of historical figures almost as if they were characters from a soap opera ensures that the reader is invested in what happens to these people. Yet, while Black successfully conveys much about what may have motivated leading figures in history, the reader is left with a one-dimensional understanding of historical events. For instance, at no point in the book does Black offer any discussion or analysis of the socio-economic contexts that played such an important role in influencing the course of history. Black's readership may be fine with that, but *Learning from History* left this reviewer wanting rather more.

Reviewer C

History has undergone quite a revival, or at least a re-branding, in recent years, with numerous books, TV series and podcasts attempting to make the subject more accessible to general audiences. Louis Black is a writer with similar ambitions and in *Learning from History*, he demonstrates a clear understanding of this core demographic. In particular, the book provides a neat overview of key figures in history, without troubling the reader unduly about details that specialists would crave. As ever, Black writes with an approachable lightness that neither alienates nor patronises his target audience whose interest in the subject may be limited to curiosity about military leaders, political figures and the odd king or two. Frustratingly, though, Black's unquestionable talent for page-turning writing is somewhat wasted in *Learning from History*. Had he turned his attention to the fascinating but complex factors that shaped historical events, it would have made the book ultimately more satisfying.

Reviewer D

Applying psychoanalytical techniques to the serious business of understanding history? It's certainly an interesting premise, and an approach that is becoming increasingly popular these days. After all, there is much to be gained from explaining the factors driving the way in which people behave in pivotal moments. Louis Black's attempts to do this in his latest book, Learning from History, by exploring the motivations of key historical leaders and the extent to which their military, political or economic policies were influenced by their psychological states of mind. However, while the opening chapters are mildly diverting, Black's tendency to make sweeping generalisations, coupled with his intimate conversational style, soon irritate. As a result, the book is unlikely to keep readers fully engrossed throughout. Nevertheless, Learning from History will certainly find an audience, presumably amongst those wishing to focus specifically on the people who have shaped our history.

Which reviewer:

has a similar opinion to Reviewer D concerning the book's intended audience?   **37**

expresses a different opinion to Reviewer D about the main aim of the book?   **38**

has a similar view to Reviewer C regarding Black's coverage of the topic?   **39**

has a different opinion to the other reviewers about the overall impact of Black's writing?   **40**

You are going to read an extract from a magazine article. Six paragraphs have been removed. Select from the paragraphs A–G the one that fits each gap (41–46). There is one extra paragraph that you do not need to use.

A Matter of Taste

As a self-avowed 'foodie', I love experimenting with different cuisines, flavours, and textures, as my extensive cookbook collection confirms. When it comes to the quality of ingredients I choose, some might call me 'snobbish', though I prefer the term 'discerning'. That's why I've always wondered whether I should work in the food industry in some capacity. In fact, I've long suspected that my true calling is as a professional food and drink taster. Am I deluded, or could my taste buds actually make the grade?

41	

This ability to identify and articulate the qualities of food is called 'sensory acuity' and is integral to how tasters assist food companies. Unsurprisingly, the taster role is far removed from my childhood dream of running amok in a food factory, gorging myself on whatever I fancy and giving my personal stamp of approval. In reality, tasters sample carefully calibrated portions before analysing and discussing their qualities in minute detail. The products are evaluated not only for flavour, but also for other sensory components, such as crunch or smoothness.

42	

This begs the question: Why does food development entail such painstaking work? Part of the reason is that tasters' judgement can help companies optimise their products for very specific markets. Consumer palates and flavour preferences tend to vary across regions, so a 'one-size-fits-all' approach rarely works in the food and beverage industry. Instead, food conglomerates launching their products worldwide will tweak their offerings to suit the particular combination of flavours that they believe will appeal to a particular target market.

43	

Encouragingly, though, Anya McDonald, a director of food testing for a multinational corporation, assures me that although a background in food science or nutrition can be advantageous, there isn't a fixed route into the profession. Prospective recruits take aptitude tests that identify those with potential. Successful candidates then undergo rigorous training designed to develop their skills further. Interestingly, professional testers, regardless of their experience or seniority, regularly undergo training to ensure that their sensory acuity hasn't diminished.

44	

This policy is one measure that food companies employ to maintain the reliability of their testing procedures. Similarly, conducting food testing using independent panels or groups also serves to ensure that decisions are consistent and as unbiased as possible. The tasters themselves have a role to play as well by taking every effort to keep their taste buds intact. They avoid spicy food wherever possible and may even refrain from wearing strong perfumes or aftershaves, since smell can substantially distort one's perception of taste.

45	

While professional tasters generally work on offerings across a company's product line, for example from savoury snacks to ice-cream, certain products involve a specialised approach due to the complexity of their flavours. Coffee, which can vary wildly based on numerous variables, is one such item. Coffee tasters are regarded as master connoisseurs, and their astounding product knowledge takes years of training to acquire. They obtain numerous qualifications to hone their skills, and their work may even involve travelling the world to learn how roasting techniques, climatic conditions and types of bean affect final products' blend of flavours.

46	

A While I have no concerns about my skills in that regard, I wonder how tasters respond when repeatedly tasting food that they dislike. Remaining impartial about food you wouldn't necessarily choose to eat yourself is surely a key requirement of the role.

B To spoil the fantasy further, tasters usually sample the same product endlessly throughout the entire development process, which can last several months. As well as the inevitable monotony, consuming excessive amounts of the same food regularly can even lead to side effects, including mouth ulcers.

C Protocols and precautions apart, professional food tasting at its most fundamental requires attention to detail and an intrinsic enthusiasm for food. With those as a starting point, the opportunities in this field are surprisingly vast. There is scope for specialisation and major international projects, especially when the product requires a high level of expertise.

D Make no mistake, not everyone possesses a palate sufficiently sensitive to make it as a professional food taster. Even those who can tune into different flavours might not necessarily be able to convey clearly the taste profiles they're experiencing.

E Admittedly, the prestige of this specialist position is attractive. Even so, I wonder whether such forensic attention to detail would eventually dampen my passion for food and drink. Better, perhaps, to remain an amateur enthusiast after all.

F Thus, tasters who are adept are pinpointing specific flavour profiles are highly sought after, and can be rewarded extremely well. I certainly pride myself on having a refined palate and being able to pick out even the subtlest of flavours. How would I fare in this profession?

G This is necessary because, like over-worked muscles, taste buds can fatigue over time. Should this occur, it would naturally impede tasters' ability to work. To avoid such a scenario, it is therefore common practice for individual tasters to work on a part-time basis.

You are going to read a magazine article in which five careers advisors discuss recruitment. For questions 47–56, select the advisor (A–E) using the separate answer sheet. The advisors may be selected more than once.

Which advisor makes the following statement?

Employers are increasingly making recruitment decisions based on a combination of methods.	**47**
Adapt your professional documentation to reflect the position you're applying for.	**48**
The methods that some companies use to learn about an applicant are questionable.	**49**
Official action has been taken to stop unfair employment practices.	**50**
The fundamental purpose of recruitment has changed for some employers.	**51**
Employers may rely on CVs to help them decide between comparable applicants.	**52**
Candidates should consider the content of their application objectively.	**53**
Regardless of current work status, it is worth working on ways to raise one's professional profile.	**54**
A company's unique environment can be detected from the way it selects its staff.	**55**
Be mindful of the type of information you make available in the public domain.	**56**

Recruitment

How are companies changing their recruitment processes? We've asked five experts to give us their insider tips on how to stand out from the crowd.

Advisor A

In some regards, modern recruitment practices are not so far removed from how companies used to select employees in the past, albeit of course that in many countries there is increasing legislation designed to protect people from discrimination. Employers need to eliminate unsuitable applicants efficiently before determining a shortlist of viable candidates. Considerable emphasis is therefore placed on academic and professional credentials even in the initial or preliminary application stages. This information will typically be scrutinised at length during the subsequent recruitment stages. As the recruitment process has changed little over the years, neither have the keys to success for job seekers. Put simply, be fully honest and never underestimate the importance of unbiased feedback. Put yourself in the position of a complete stranger: what issues are likely to arise from the claims you have made in your application?

Advisor B

While most companies continue to use CVs for initial vetting, many employers now acknowledge the limitations of the traditional 'application form, then interview' recruitment model. Certainly, in some sectors companies may supplement these conventional recruitment practices with alternative ways of ascertaining how prospective candidates would fare in their particular corporate environment. Such techniques could involve problem-solving simulations or practical tasks, both of which arguably providing more reliable evidence of a candidate's true abilities. But, as a potential employee, these methods can also give *you* a more accurate insight into a company's specific ethos and corporate culture. It's worth reflecting honestly on your feelings throughout the entire recruitment process. What did the experience reveal about working for that particular company? Remember that recruitment should be a two-way process.

Advisor C

When it comes to standing out from the crowd in fiercely competitive job markets, the expression 'first impressions count' is worth heeding. CVs are typically the first thing that companies see when making hiring decisions, and they can play a pivotal role in differentiating between similarly qualified candidates. They are at their most effective when they promote key skills and qualities rather than simply listing a person's professional background or academic achievements. For this reason, CVs should be customised every time they are submitted. Analyse the core requirements of a particular role and then tailor the style, layout and content of your CV accordingly. Sections of key pertinence or particular strength should take prime position to put the spotlight on exactly what you can offer.

Advisor D

People with their sights set firmly on securing one particular dream role often have a clear idea of what their potential employer requires. However, recruitment is no longer simply about selecting an applicant for a specific role. Nowadays, many corporate employers actually use it instead to discover the pool of talent available, before then determining how they can best utilise the most outstanding individuals in their company. That's why professionals at any stage of their career can benefit from 'personal marketing'. Even if they are not actively searching for a new position, professionals should continue to develop their personal brand online, and promote themselves at every possible opportunity. This can create exciting new openings, while also raising their profile and value in their current workplace.

Advisor E

As well as actively engaging with professional networking communities and sites, many ambitious professionals launch their own websites, blogs and social media channels. This builds visibility within their industry, improving the likelihood that potential employers will reach out to them. These tools convey a carefully crafted public persona, but what about personal online accounts? Nowadays, companies may browse non-work social media posts, either to evaluate the suitability of a prospective candidate or investigate concerns they may have about an employee's conduct. We might challenge the ethics of this, but, even so, online content can often be found with astonishing ease. So-called reputation-management companies can analyse the entire history of an individual's digital footprint in forensic detail and can remove, or at least hide, undesirable elements. However, professionals are advised to think twice about what they share online, and who can access it.

Name _____   Date _____

Part 5

Mark the appropriate answer (A, B, C or D).

0	A	B	C▬	D

31	A	B	C	D		34	A	B	C	D
32	A	B	C	D		35	A	B	C	D
33	A	B	C	D		36	A	B	C	D

Part 6

Add the appropriate answer (A–D).

37	38	39	40

Part 7

Add the appropriate answer (A–G).

41	42	43
44	45	46

Part 8

Add the appropriate answer (A–E).

47	48	49	50	51
52	53	54	55	56

www.prosperityeducation.net

Cambridge C1 Advanced
Reading: Parts 5–8

Test 5

You are going to read an article in which the writer discusses sleep. For questions 31–36, mark the appropriate answer (A, B, C or D) that you think fits best according to the text.

Understanding the Sleep Crisis

Professor James Windsor surveys the issue of sleep deprivation in contemporary society.

Media reports concerning the nation's sleep habits hardly make for relaxing bedtime reading. Items warning readers about the mental and physical effects of sleep loss are becoming commonplace, which in turn spawns endless articles in lifestyle magazines about the issue. These articles urge readers to improve their 'sleep hygiene', yet offer strategies rarely more insightful than avoiding caffeine at night. For those seeking additional support, commercial solutions are never far away. We are bombarded with advertisements promoting a raft of sleep-enhancing products, from traditional herbal remedies to meditative podcasts and orthopaedic mattresses. Of course, some of the more sensationalist content the public is exposed to may well be driven by a desire to monetise people's bedtime routines. However, worrying headlines about society's 'sleep crisis' should not be viewed simply as media hype. Experts are finding convincing evidence that sleep deprivation is rife and its impacts severe.

Sleep crisis is indeed a fitting term, given that researchers are reporting on multiple areas of concern. Firstly, serious sleep disorders, such as sleep apnoea or parasomnia are reputedly on the rise. These debilitating disorders mean that, for a growing number of people, sleep is anything but restorative. As is becoming increasingly clear, sleep disorders can lead to significant physical problems, not to mention undoubted increases in mental and emotional stress. This makes it all the more unfathomable that TV producers think it is wise to exploit these disorders for comedic effect or present them as a quirk to reinforce a character's eccentricity. In light of this, the sooner sleep conditions are moved up the healthcare agenda, the better.

Not that society's sleep issues are confined to specific sleep disorders. It is no secret that sleep is intrinsic to our mental and physical wellbeing, which is why scientists and healthcare professionals argue that society's fundamental relationship with sleep deserves a rethink. The research to back this up is clear. Whether it has come about by accident or by design, one key point is at least certain: there has been an indisputable decrease in adults' sleep-quality levels, a downward trend dating back decades. Adults are sleeping quantifiably less than was once the norm, and in many cases, significantly so. Moreover, sleep deprivation is becoming especially prevalent amongst children and adolescents, the very individuals that need restful sleep the most.

Studies on sleep patterns are generally conducted with reference to the ideal amount of sleep recommended by the World Health Organization (WHO), namely eight hours a night. A distinction should be drawn between this benchmark and arbitrary targets used in some public-health campaigns. When educating the public about making healthier lifestyle choices, there is a tendency to promote the overall message using quantifiable, achievable goals. The specific numbers matter less than encouraging positive behavioural change, such as eating more vegetables or walking more. By contrast, the 'eight hours' threshold is based on sound medical research, and represents the actual sleep requirement of an average adult. While factors such as age and physical build may affect individual sleep requirements, this will only vary within an extremely limited range. Putting aside a tiny number of people with certain genetic disorders, it is a myth that dropping below or 'getting by' on seven hours' sleep is safe.

Unsurprisingly, poor sleeping habits are often attributed to contemporary lifestyles. However, rather than addressing the problem, too many individuals focus instead on changing things that they believe are easier to control, like their dietary choices. Furthermore, nutrition can never make up for the serious effects of sleep deprivation. Likewise, when companies use hectic lifestyles as justification for products like under-eye cream or energy drinks, it is hardly surprising that sleep deprivation is viewed as little more than a minor inconvenience. More harmful yet are the boastful claims public figures make about how little they themselves sleep. Presenting a lack of sleep as a badge of honour sends the deeply insidious message that successful people simply do not need to bother with such insignificant matters as sleep.

Fortunately, there are signs that the message may finally be getting through. Particularly encouraging is the progress being made in terms of making work and school schedules more conducive to healthy sleep routines. Ultimately, addressing the root causes of sleep deprivation necessitates a fundamental shift in thinking by individuals and society as a whole.

31 In the first paragraph, the writer suggests that media coverage of sleep loss is mainly:

    A lacking in depth

    B persuasive to readers

    C commercially motivated

    D justifiably negative.

32 What does the writer imply about sleep disorders in the second paragraph?

    A More emphasis should be placed on their psychological impacts.

    B The way they are portrayed in the public domain can be harmful.

    C They are more common than is generally believed.

    D Public understanding of them is limited.

33 In the third paragraph, the writer expresses uncertainty about:

    A how the problem of sleep deprivation affects society

    B which groups in society experience the most sleep deprivation

    C whether studies on sleep deprivation can alter people's attitudes

    D why people's sleep habits appear to have changed.

34 What point is made about the recommended sleep guideline of eight hours a night?

    A It is designed mainly to educate people about the importance of sleep.

    B It represents a total that is realistic rather than optimal.

    C The safe margin of variation around this total is surprisingly narrow.

    D It is conceptually similar to daily exercise targets.

35 What attitude is the writer most critical of in the fifth paragraph?

    A Prioritising sleep is a sign of weakness.

    B A healthy diet can compensate for poor sleep.

    C Modern lifestyles make sleep loss inevitable.

    D Developing better sleep habits is a challenge.

36 What is the overall aim of the text?

    A To correct some misconceptions about an issue.

    B To draw attention to an issue.

    C To discuss the implications of an issue.

    D To evaluate different approaches to an issue.

You are going to read four extracts from articles in which academics discuss artificial intelligence (AI). For questions 37–40, choose from the academics A–D. The academics may be selected more than once. Mark your answers on the separate answer sheet.

Artificial Intelligence

Academic A

All too often, AI is portrayed in films and TV shows as a sinister force posing a threat to humanity. The implication is that if we enable machines to 'think' and take decisions, then there is a possibility that these machines will eventually rise up against us. Even serious journalists frame their discussions of AI using provocative questions, such as 'Will AI take over the world?' Even if the content of the articles themselves is measured and balanced, the damage is done by their typically attention-grabbing headlines. However, machine learning, which is the foundation of AI, is not the same as human thought or intellect. The most common form of machine learning merely involves programming machines to perform tasks or make decisions automatically by searching for specific patterns in data. Automated systems, like light sensors or online booking systems, are prime examples of this, highlighting the actual reality of AI.

Academic B

'Narrow AI' forms the majority of the AI applications we currently have at our disposal, and is concerned with automating tasks that are, conceptually, relatively simple. Humans can already detect faults in pipelines, recognise particular faces in an image, or spot inappropriate content on a website. However, AI enables computerised systems to accomplish these things far more quickly. Narrow AI will certainly become further embedded in our daily lives without controversy. By contrast, the prospect of 'general AI' attracts far more debate. It has captured the public's imagination and certainly raises interesting philosophical questions. General AI is about the development of super-intelligent machines able to evaluate, adapt and take decisions without input from humans. As this resembles human thought, public fears are understandable. However, if general AI is eventually possible, superintelligence will never lead to sentient machines. Actually, a far more pressing concern is whether humans will use general AI responsibly and sensibly.

Academic C

AI is not destined to evolve into a malevolent force beyond human control, and at the risk of offending sci-fi fans or media outlets, that harmful misconception is largely due to the way in which the subject is treated in public discourse. AI is not to be feared, nor should machine learning be confused with human thought. Computerised chess simulations are able to beat humans simply because they have the processing ability to calculate the possible outcomes of thousands of different moves. However, their decisions are still governed by fixed, predictable rules. While AI has progressed to the extent that machines can now outperform us in many ways, it does not follow from this that human survival is at stake. Instead, as AI tools develop further, it is worth considering how these exciting advances may shape society in the future. For instance, how will AI impact on aspects like employment?

Academic D

I'm inclined to concede that AI lacks the flexibility or adaptability of thought associated with human cognition. That's certainly the case at present with the so-called narrow AI tools we use for a range of purposes. That said, the prospect of general AI, which is yet to happen, of course, may involve deeper types of learning. Even so, the outcome will not be machines with the capacity to experience emotions. And unlike humans, super-intelligent machines will probably never be able to immediately respond to data without numerous iterations of trial-and-error experimentation. Of course, this doesn't mean that the development of AI is without its risks. Ultimately, the future of AI and, more importantly, the consequences for society is in our hands. As AI technology progresses, we need to ensure that we develop these tools in the right way. If we are careless or, worse, unethical in their application, the consequences could be far-reaching and disastrous.

Which academic:

expresses a similar view to Academic C regarding the influence of media coverage of AI?

| 37 | |

has a different opinion to the others about whether machine learning is similar to the way in which humans process information?

| 38 | |

expresses a similar view to Academic B concerning a distinction to be made between the different types of AI?

| 39 | |

shares a similar view to Academic D concerning how humans will play a role in future AI development?

| 40 | |

Pitch Perfect!

Josh Hawkins describes his experience of the Business Brains competition

I am probably not the image that naturally springs to mind when picturing a student entrepreneur. For one thing, I'm not a business student, and I have no background knowledge of finance or marketing. They are most definitely not part of the syllabus for my art degree, and, until last month, I'd never even seen a profit–loss spreadsheet before. Nor am I a particularly confident speaker. To be honest, I'm the last person you'd expect to see pitching an idea for a start-up.

| 41 | |

When I initially entered, I wasn't really expecting to progress very far, but I hoped that the experience itself would be useful. While I had the seed of an idea about creating personalised gifts and cards, I didn't know how to turn this into a viable business. Therefore, I reasoned that entering the competition would not only help me develop some practical new skills, but also be exactly the impetus I needed to stop dreaming and actually do something.

| 42 | |

If all that weren't daunting enough, this multi-round format means students have to juggle their competition preparation with their existing academic commitments. This is a real-life lesson about the importance of time management! Fortunately, the university provides excellent guidance to entrants via mentors. These mentors offer practical advice on the core concepts that students from a non-business background might be unfamiliar with. Even better, no matter how far students go during the heats, they can continue to consult the mentors after the competition.

| 43 | |

This collaborative mentality makes sense. Although the university does grant a small sum to one overall winner, the main purpose is for students to gain exposure and find investors for their ideas. *Business Brains* generates considerable interest from local investors with a range of expertise in various sectors. These investors are keen to discover the next great idea, and there's a high chance that any participant whose business plan is strong enough to get through the initial elimination rounds will win some form of financial backing.

| 44 | |

Obviously, the purpose of this isn't to undermine students' enthusiasm. Instead, the point is that even if you believe your idea is bound to succeed, what concrete evidence can you provide to convince investors? After all, when you are so emotionally invested in something, it can be difficult to appraise it objectively. Likewise, loved ones often just say what they think you want to hear! The feedback from your *Business Brains* peers and mentors genuinely helps you analyse your idea from fresh perspectives.

| 45 | |

One such element is 'proof of concept', which essentially means showing that your idea is feasible, and that there is actual demand for it. For instance, I could prove there was demand for my personalised gifts and cards. As soon as I started making them for university friends, word of mouth spread. Soon, I was receiving requests from complete strangers, all begging to order bespoke gifts from me. This demonstrated that my creations were popular, and that people were willing to pay for them.

| 46 | |

A The other aspect I found incredibly beneficial was preparing my business plan. Completing this document clarified the specific steps involved in launching a business. It also gave me an understanding of exactly what entrepreneurs need to demonstrate when pitching to investors.

B With all this encouragement, *Business Brains* is more like a hands-on work experience placement than a competition. At every stage of the process, participants help and learn from their peers, rather than treat one another as rivals. This truly brings out the best in everyone.

C Yet, that is exactly what I had to do as part of the university's annual *Business Brains* competition. Deciding to take the plunge and apply was a huge leap into the unknown for me, but I'm so glad that I did.

D From this perspective, I thought I had a decent chance of progressing to the final, but getting that confirmation was overwhelming. I was so nervous during my pitch, but, even so, I received several offers of investment, which was incredible. Entering the *Business Brains* competition has definitely been the smartest decision I've ever made!

E The competition involves presenting your business plan to a panel of experts. It's so inspiring to see fellow students pitching their ideas. Many of the participants, even those who didn't win, have gone on to launch successful businesses.

F The competition certainly forces students to go beyond the basic idea stage. In the first heats, entrants are required to develop an actual business plan. The best entrants are selected to continue to the final round, which involves presenting their ideas to potential investors.

G Of course, getting to that point is far easier said than done, despite all the support on hand. Participants have their ideas scrutinised from every possible angle, and must be prepared to address any issues that arise during this process.

You are going to read a newspaper column in which five residents give their opinions about city-centre traffic congestion. For questions 47–56, select the resident (A–E) using the separate answer sheet. The residents may be selected more than once.

Which local resident makes the following statement?

Traffic-calming measures have a direct impact on the city's economy.	**47**
Actions that punish people are not the most effective way to address traffic congestion.	**48**
Highlighting the environmental benefits is the key to the proposal's success.	**49**
The local authorities are starting to take the problem of traffic in the city seriously.	**50**
The proposal is likely to be popular with most local people.	**51**
The positives of the initiative outweigh the negatives.	**52**
Local businesses should be consulted on traffic-calming measures.	**53**
Placing specific limits on the number of cars is difficult to implement.	**54**
People mainly drive into the city out of necessity rather than preference.	**55**
Traffic-calming measures rarely have a major impact in real terms on actual traffic levels.	**56**

Traffic Congestion

How should traffic congestion in the city centre be tackled? We've asked five local residents to give us their views about the local council's latest traffic-calming proposals.

Resident A

Clearly, action needs to be taken to address our horrendous rush-hour traffic. Our city is the region's principal economic hub, so traffic congestion is inevitable if the underlying infrastructure is inadequate. That's why I find it frustrating that whenever 'traffic calming' is discussed, the blame is placed solely on motorists. As far as I'm concerned, the core problem is the lack of viable public-transport alternatives. Without these, what are commuters, residents and shoppers supposed to do? Tinkering around with half-measures like pedestrianised streets, one-way traffic routes and more stringent parking fines only serve to add to people's frustration. If the council truly wants to dissuade people from using their cars, positive incentives are far more likely to lead to desirable outcomes than simply focusing on punitive measures.

Resident B

City-centre businesses and traders provide employment for local people, and generate high levels of revenue for the local economy. Their voices should be heard on important local issues because these stakeholders can offer useful insights into what matters to city residents and visitors to the city alike. Council policy regarding traffic into and out of the city is a prime example. We know that city-centre vehicle bans significantly reduce the number of people entering the city to shop or use the local amenities. This may make the city centre safer for pedestrians and cyclists, but the obvious effect on the city's commercial opportunities must not be overlooked. More investment in bus routes and underground trains would be a welcome addition to the city while also alleviating traffic congestion in the centre.

Resident C

Apparently, the council wants to create vehicle-free zones in the city centre. To be honest, I've yet to be convinced about the merits of this. Similar policies have been trialled before, and they were all eventually abandoned because the effect that they had on the volume of traffic was negligible. All they do is move the congestion elsewhere. They don't change people's habits in any meaningful way. Instead, motorists simply leave their cars in residential areas, increasing the disruption there. As a resident in one such suburb, I'm dreading the inevitable impact on my neighbourhood. That said, I shall concede that, at least this time, the council will impose considerably harsher fines for any traffic violations. But, while the council is committed to addressing the issue, there must be better ways to do it.

Resident D

Any traffic-calming plan is bound to be unpopular at first, but it must be worth pursuing if it promises to reduce the number of vehicles in the city centre. Traffic jams are getting worse, as is air quality in this city. Nothing is going to improve unless the council takes action. There is so much to be gained from the proposal. For instance, it could be the impetus that will finally persuade people to use public transport, or cycle more. Of course, in the long term, the plan will only work if the public supports it. Emphasising the reduction in air pollution is likely to be the best way to achieve this support. Surely, this, combined with safer, more peaceful cities, makes any minor inconvenience to motorists a price worth paying.

Resident E

I'm inclined to support a total ban on cars in the city centre. I accept that it might have implications for local businesses, but the vast majority of people around here will embrace the measure. For this reason, I'm pleased that the council has committed itself to moving ahead with the initiative. Some people are calling for alternative measures instead, such as introducing vehicle-quota schemes. This approach is about controlling the total number of vehicles at any given time, which would certainly help to relieve traffic congestion. For instance, in some towns and cities, a prescribed number of vehicles can enter urban areas on particular days, or at certain times during each day. I'm less keen on this suggestion, because it seems impractical and wouldn't fundamentally change people's attitudes to driving.

Name _____

Date _____

Part 5

Mark the appropriate answer (A, B, C or D).

0	A	B	C	D	

31	A	B	C	D		34	A	B	C	D
32	A	B	C	D		35	A	B	C	D
33	A	B	C	D		36	A	B	C	D

Part 6

Add the appropriate answer (A–D).

37		38		39		40	

Part 7

Add the appropriate answer (A–G).

41		42		43	
44		45		46	

Part 8

Add the appropriate answer (A–E).

47		48		49		50		51	
52		53		54		55		56	

PROSPERITY EDUCATION
www.prosperityeducation.net

Cambridge C1 Advanced
Reading: Parts 5–8

Test 6

You are going to read an introduction to a book about deception. For questions 31–36, mark the appropriate answer (A, B, C or D) that you think fits best according to the text.

On Deception

Last year, I gladly accepted a magazine assignment about deception. I was delighted to write about such a simple topic having spent months grappling with the intricacies of the absorbing but highly charged subjects of culture and identity politics for my debut book. Indeed, my only initial reservation was whether I would find enough ideas to write about. After all, though we may justify white lies for pragmatic reasons, society's disapproval of lying is relatively clear-cut. Deception is, as Aeschylus wrote over two thousand years ago, the 'foulest plague of all'. While that may be something of an exaggeration to modern readers, the sentiment still resonates, albeit in less absolutist terms.

Any misapprehensions about the paucity of the topic were dispelled when I began researching the mechanics of lying. Perhaps 'the art of lying' may be a better term. For some, it is surely a talent. These people seem to possess an innate ability to deceive, embodying the proverbial 'born liar'. On the other hand, many of us pride ourselves on being able to spot deception. When facing a person with such a propensity for falsehood, the received wisdom is to pay close attention to their body language. Paralinguistic information is believed to reveal a speaker's true feelings, with nose-scratching and lack of eye contact commonly cited as sure-fire signs of falsehood. However, that and so many other assumptions about dishonesty are open to debate, which is why what began as a magazine article evolved into the present book.

Uncovering deceit is anything but straightforward, despite what pseudo-scientific lifestyle magazines may claim. Studies of people's ability to detect evasion have revealed that success rates within the general population are so low as to be, for all intents and purposes, a random coin toss. Even those who have been highly trained find it difficult to detect deceit with complete accuracy. Within the justice system, for instance, professional lie detection can have potentially life-changing consequences. Therefore, when TV talk shows use lie-detecting tests (polygraph) as a form of entertainment to settle petty domestic squabbles, it belittles the vital work done by psychologists and law enforcers.

While psychology has by no means identified definitive hallmarks of dishonesty, researchers are gaining more insights into the nature of deceit and so-called deception cues. There is evidence that a high-pitched voice can indeed betray a liar's guilt. Yet, research is actually debunking pervasive myths, too. The notion that liars employ excessive gesticulation has been shown to be wide of the mark; liars actually fidget less than those telling the truth. Caution should also be applied when making judgements about someone's honesty based on eye contact alone. Only in extremely high-stakes situations have liars been found to avoid a person's gaze. Research also reveals the traits that are more likely to yield negative impressions from others. Although the evidence is mixed on whether hesitation is an accurate predictor of deception, it is frequently viewed as such, with potentially far-reaching implications in judicial contexts.

A more fruitful line of enquiry for researchers may be in the analysis of what a person says, rather than how they say it. Encouragingly, computer software can search written samples for qualifying devices, negative language or impersonal language, all of which have been identified as deception cues. Such language can, of course, betray liars in speaking, too, underlining the importance of how interviews are conducted in high-stakes situations. With effective training, interviewers can hone in on linguistic cues that, when taken in conjunction with other evidence, may provide a more complete picture of a person's state of mind. It is equally important that they build rapport with their interviewees, thereby improving the likelihood of eliciting fuller samples to analyse.

Though the present book focuses on the psychology of deception, no prior knowledge is assumed on the part of the reader. It should also be underlined that ethical issues are debated only insofar as they illuminate how research findings on deception may have broader social implications. Those hoping to delve into the moral quandaries of lying may be surprised, as will those expecting a degree of polemical debate. Instead, in the following pages, I strive to cast an objectively scientific eye on the subject, and I hope my loyal readers will find the resulting book no less interesting for that.

31 The writer refers to a quotation from Aeschylus to show that:

    A   dishonesty has seldom been perceived in a positive light

    B   ancient and contemporary attitudes towards dishonesty differ

    C   the subject of dishonesty involves complex moral issues

    D   culture affects attitudes towards dishonesty.

32 In the second paragraph, the writer express scepticism about the notion that:

    A   people regard themselves as good judges of character

    B   people have a natural inclination for lying

    C   deception can be regarded as a skill

    D   non-verbal clues are reliable indicators of deception.

33 The writer refers to tossing a coin to highlight that:

    A   media outlets trivialise the field of lie detection

    B   people struggle to detect lies accurately

    C   training has a negligible effect on lie detection rates

    D   lie detection is viewed as unscientific as a field.

34 According to the research mentioned in the fourth paragraph, liars are most likely to:

    A   be slow to give responses

    B   make fidgeting hand gestures

    C   avoid eye contact

    D   speak at a higher pitch.

35 What point does the writer make about lie detection methods in the fifth paragraph?

    A   Computers can detect lies more effectively than humans can.

    B   Interviewers can influence a person's responses.

    C   Lies are easier to detect in writing than in speaking.

    D   Language choice rather than delivery reveals more about deception.

36 From the final paragraph, it can be inferred that the writer's earlier works have:

    A   focused on scientific themes

    B   overlooked research-based evidence

    C   presented personal stances

    D   attracted specialist audiences.

You are going to read four reviews about a theatre play. For questions 37–40, choose from the reviewers A–D. The reviewers may be selected more than once. Mark your answers on the separate answer sheet.

Spotlight on: *F*

Four reviewers comment on *F*, Max Astley's latest theatrical offering

Reviewer A

The enigmatically titled *F* demonstrates that Max Astley is a playwright and director approaching the very peak of his creative powers. Drawing on ancient Norse myths and legends, *F* covers familiar ground exploring the corrosive power of jealousy and revenge. The use of mythology as a story-telling device may have been done before, but rarely with such humour or lightness. Talking of lightness, Liza Hammond and Helen Baines are both hilarious, while Louis Chapman is a revelation. Of course, the popularity of these high-profile stars was almost certainly a consideration in Astley's casting, but there is no shame in that providing the performers can deliver. Fortunately for Astley, all three prove themselves to be naturally gifted stage performers. They make the substantial running time fly by, and at no point does one's attention drift. Both they and Astley thoroughly deserve the praise heading their way from sceptical reviewers.

Reviewer B

From the casting of three extremely well-known figures from the world of television to the excessive use of popular culture references, Max Astley signals his desire to conquer contemporary theatre in his latest play. Astley's outstanding reputation as a director and playwright is known, yet so far plaudits away from the staid world of classical theatre have eluded him. However, this looks set to change with his latest play, *F*. Essentially an exploration of the power dynamics in family relationships, Astley's treatment of the subject is fresh, with an unusual plot, and the performances are entertaining. Helen Baines' turn as the sardonic Mary is a particular highlight. At times her presence injects vitality into a meandering final act that should have been significantly shorter. In fact, *F* would have been snappier had it been pruned throughout. Minor quibbles aside, *F* shows Astley's versatility and skill as a contemporary playwright.

Reviewer C

In a play full of flashy gimmicks, it would be easy to dismiss Max Astley's casting decisions as yet another attention-grabbing publicity tactic. The fact that he overlooked a wealth of established theatre actors in favour of TV performers with a wider public fanbase is a certainly controversial one, but by no means is this the main shortcoming of *F*. In truth, the performers are more than competent, especially given the lack of inspiring material to deliver. The reality is that the underlying fault lies squarely with Astley's dull content. He is guilty of trying to do too much, and in so doing, ends up achieving little. The play lacks direction or even an original story. For instance, the sections based on Norse legends neither add anything to the main plot nor linger long in the memory. Why Astley chose to call the play *F* is unclear, but for this reviewer at least, it stands for the rating it deserves.

Reviewer D

Max Astley certainly could not be accused of being a playwright lacking in ambition. In the highly enjoyable *F*, he takes us on a whistle-stop tour of ancient Norse mythology woven into the principal plot of a power struggle between estranged siblings. The play barely pauses for breath in what feels like a remarkably short three hours. If that sounds exhausting for the audience, pity the performers; all three of them. The immense demands placed on them make Astley's choice of actors all the more inspired. In the run-up to its premiere, most of the speculation about *F* concerned the decision to cast performers primarily known as TV presenters rather than established theatre actors. There's no doubt that Astley knew the interest this would generate. In the arts, there's no such thing as 'bad publicity'. In truth, the casting is perfect. *F*'s pace and Astley's naturalistic dialogue capture the feeling of live television at its best.

Which reviewer:

has a different opinion to the other reviewers regarding Astley's motives when selecting the cast?	**37**
expresses a different opinion to Reviewer D concerning the length of the play?	**38**
has a similar view to Reviewer B about whether the play will be popular with critics?	**39**
has a similar opinion to Reviewer A about the uniqueness of the plot?	**40**

You are going to read an extract from a blog post. Six paragraphs have been removed. Select from the paragraphs A–G the one that fits each gap (41–46). There is one extra paragraph that you do not need to use.

Sustainable Tourism

As a blogger, I make my living doing the thing I love most in the world, namely travelling. What started as an outlet to share travel experiences with fellow globetrotters has become a full-time career. Working with travel brands in a professional capacity affords me the opportunity to explore places I may not have had the financial means to visit under my own steam. I'm fully aware of what an incredible privilege this is, but that doesn't mean I view the travel industry through rose-tinted glasses.

41

Whether this makes me a hypocrite is for others to judge, but I will always endeavour to hold the travel industry to account while using my platform to actively promote sustainable forms of tourism. But of course, this doesn't leave travellers themselves off the hook. We all need to ensure that local communities are not negatively affected by our wanderlust, and, at the same time, policy-makers and authorities have their part to play by introducing more stringent controls on tourism.

42

This is because, without a doubt, when left unchecked, tourism can certainly wreak havoc on historical sites, spots of natural beauty and villages whose infrastructures simply cannot cope with large influxes of people. Sadly, environmental and cultural degradation are the hallmarks of areas blighted by uncontrolled tourism. Yet, authorities grappling with this issue face a dilemma: there is understandable reluctance to impose restrictions so draconian that they permanently alienate tourists and harm the local economy. However, half-hearted measures are simply too lax to be effective.

43

This quantitative approach seeks to make tourism less harmful by focusing predominantly on preventing overcrowding. After all, if there are fewer people in a place at any given time, there will be less pollution, traffic congestion and rubbish to contend with. It also reduces the damage to crumbling ancient ruins, or fragile ecosystems. While the tourist boom shows no sign of abating, some of the world's most celebrated sites have started to set upper caps on visitor numbers, often with impressive results.

44

Of course, such restrictions make it imperative for travellers to plan ahead in order to avoid running the risk of being turned away. As frustrating as this may be for people whose travel itineraries afford them limited flexibility, quotas can be an essential way to protect tourist destinations before it is too late. Sadly, instead of embracing the rules, some travel companies or individuals try to circumvent the restrictions in some way. It is precisely this selfish attitude that lies at the heart of the problem with mass tourism.

45

This has already happened in some coastal resorts worldwide. In Thailand, for instance, the surge in tourism in the early 2000s resulted in endless throngs of motor boats zipping across bays, causing untold harm to the stunning coral reefs beneath. Authorities had to take the unpopular decision of closing these beaches entirely for months at a time in a bid to restore marine life. When given the chance, coral reefs can regenerate, but having to resort to bans to facilitate this underlines the extent of the problem.

46

A There is cause for optimism in this particular case because the decision seems to be having the desired effect on marine life. However, the message is clear: we must all ensure that profit is never prioritised over the planet.

B Indeed, action at this macro level is key to shaping how tourism evolves in the future. Governments and councils must take appropriate measures to ensure that local communities and, of course, the environment are protected from the worst ravages of tourism.

C One such success story is Peru's renowned Inca Trail to Machu Pichu. Decades of uncontrolled tourism had jeopardised the trails and surrounding forests. Peru now strictly controls the number of tourists admitted to the site, making it easier to carry out essential conservation work. This iconic UNESCO World Cultural Heritage Site's future now looks far rosier.

D Fortunately, authorities have several tools at their disposal. For instance, visitor quotas can strike a suitable balance between welcoming tourism while lessening its negative impact. Instituting fixed limits on the number of visitors relieves pressure on tourist sites, making them more pleasant for all concerned.

E Far from it. I'm keenly aware of the ethical and environmental problems that tourism can create, or at least exacerbate. That's why, in this blog, I regularly call for more responsible actions on the part of hoteliers, airlines and tour providers.

F I also reject the argument that imposing controls compromises the adventurous spirit of independent travel, where itineraries are made and changed according to whim. Nor is ignorance an excuse to circumvent the rules. It has never been easier to find out about any restrictions in operation.

G That may sound harsh, but when communities cannot rely on the support of travellers and the tourist industry to act responsibly, the next logical step is to bar visitors altogether. Such drastic action may be the only chance of saving some areas.

You are going to read a magazine in which design experts give their opinions about interior design. For questions 47–56, select the expert (A–E) using the separate answer sheet. The experts may be selected more than once.

Which expert makes the following statement?

Incorporating cohesive style elements makes a space feel harmonious.	**47**
The function of a space should dictate the type of materials to be used.	**48**
Contemporary interior design is at its peak.	**49**
Interior design rules are rooted in principles taken from other fields.	**50**
Excessive adherence to design rules may spoil the feeling of a room.	**51**
The overall impact of colours in a space can be manipulated.	**52**
Successful interior design starts by considering the end user.	**53**
Interior design is gaining more legitimacy.	**54**
People are becoming more adventurous in their choice of interior design schemes.	**55**
Light should be a core consideration when planning a design scheme.	**56**

Rooms for Improvement!

What makes a domestic space welcoming or stylish? We've asked five interior designers to share their tricks of the trade.

Expert A

There are some basic design principles that, if you're so inclined, you could follow and you wouldn't go too far wrong. However, people shouldn't slavishly follow rules if they don't make sense in terms of their own personal aesthetic or the environment. That said, it's always important to build the design of an interior based on the amount of natural light in the space. Even the most beautifully planned interiors will look uninspiring or drab in dark rooms. Think about how the room looks at different times of the day before opting for a particular colour scheme. Similarly, consider how you plan to use the room. Delicate fabrics aren't a sensible option for the main hubs of activity because they will have to withstand a lot of wear and tear. Opt instead for something sturdier.

Expert B

Not long so ago, few people took risks or stamped their individuality on domestic spaces because they were frightened of standing out. Generally, people felt obliged to stick to neutral colour schemes and understated designs because they wanted their homes to appeal to the masses, purely for resale purposes. I'm glad that people's attitudes are changing. People are now willing to take a more experimental approach to how they decorate their homes. Lifestyle magazines and social media accounts have played a key role in encouraging people to try out new ideas for themselves. I also think that iconic TV shows can be very influential in terms of design trends that capture people's imaginations. Whatever the inspiration, we're entering a golden age of interior design, and I for one hope it continues.

Expert C

As with anything, trends in interior design come and go, and it's fascinating to see how interiors reflect changes in society. For instance, as foreign travel has become more popular, many people have become inspired to try to recreate the look and feel of exotic destinations in their own homes. At the same time, people are starting to respect the skills involved in interior design, and now recognise that it should be viewed in the same way as other creative fields. Interestingly, though, many of the core elements of effective design actually take their cue from established scientific principles. For instance, the popular 'rule of three' idea about grouping objects in groups of threes derives from psychology: this is the optimal number that the brain can process at a time.

Expert D

When I discuss design ideas with my clients, I often refer to the 'language' of interior design. Too many people focus on matching colours, when in fact they should focus on tying the overall style of the room together. This is the key to achieving balance in a space. For instance, a blue Art Deco lamp won't work in a blue, industrial-chic room because these two styles evoke completely different moods. As long as you keep this principle in mind, there's plenty of scope to experiment with different patterns, colours and fabrics. In fact, textiles are a great way of emphasising certain colours in a design or toning them down. For instance, soft furnishings with bold prints can be used to complement the main colour.

Expert E

Too many people are overly fixated on the idea of 'good taste', or whether a space will appeal to others on an aesthetic level. This leads them to prioritise conformity over individuality. However, rooms should be designed for the person(s) using them, not as an aspirational message to others. If we can't express our innermost feelings in our own homes, where can we? Worrying too much about whether a room is 'right' is a recipe for disaster. For instance, some people make the mistake of meticulously matching every colour and object in the room in an attempt to obey the interior design principle of harmony and balance. They have a misguided belief that following a specific framework will create a successful design. In reality, and all too often, it simply results in a sterile room.

Name _____   Date _____

Part 5

Mark the appropriate answer (A, B, C or D).

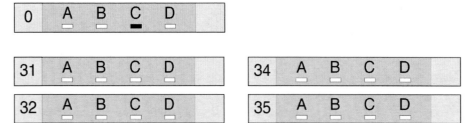

0	A	B	C	D

31	A	B	C	D		34	A	B	C	D
32	A	B	C	D		35	A	B	C	D
33	A	B	C	D		36	A	B	C	D

Part 6

Add the appropriate answer (A–D).

37	38	39	40

Part 7

Add the appropriate answer (A–G).

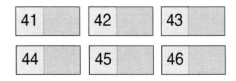

41	42	43
44	45	46

Part 8

Add the appropriate answer (A–E).

47	48	49	50	51
52	53	54	55	56

PROSPERITY EDUCATION
www.prosperityeducation.net

Cambridge C1 Advanced
Reading: Parts 5–8

Test 7

You are going to read a review of a book about friendship. For questions 31–36, mark the appropriate answer (A, B, C or D) that you think fits best according to the text.

On Friendship, by Rebecca Palmer

What's in a name? For Rebecca Palmer the answer is much, at least when people describe their relationships with various people in their social networks. In the first section of *On Friendship*, Palmer is preoccupied with the connotations of various friendship terms such as 'mate', 'chum' or 'acquaintance'. Not that the point lacks merit. Who bestows a 'best friend' moniker on someone they have just met, or assigns the term in broadly even in the nebulous context of online relationships? Nevertheless, Palmer labours the point, insisting that the decision to use 'pal' as opposed to 'chum' must automatically be an intentional and meaningful one, denoting very specific, if subtle, shades of meaning. Curiously, she fails to acknowledge the vast number of people who use friendship terms interchangeably, or whose language may be influenced by regional factors or indeed simple stylistic preferences.

If Palmer can be accused of oversimplification when discussing friendship nomenclature, the same criticism cannot be levelled elsewhere in *On Friendship*, her ambitious debut book on human relationships. Part memoir, part treatise, *On Friendship* weaves together the personal, political and philosophical to build an impassioned case for a re-evaluation of friendship in the twenty-first century. Palmer covers new ground by asserting how contemporary socio-economic structures are transforming the very nature of our social bonds. To this end, a substantial portion of the book is concerned with how schools are intentionally steering children towards certain types of friendship hierarchies.

In examining attitudes to friendship, the book gives as much credence to the views of philosophers from antiquity as those of contemporary commentators. Notably, Palmer highlights how the demarcation of friendships is far from a modern phenomenon. Indeed, Aristotle believed all friendships fell into one of three distinct categories. His so-called 'utility' friendships predicated on perceived usefulness and mutual benefit are familiar to anyone that establishes cordial terms with colleagues or neighbours for the practical advantages this may confer. Friendships 'of pleasure' resemble the friendships we have with people with whom we share a particular interest. Moreover, the concept of deeper and more meaningful friendships, the Aristotelian ideal of the friendship 'of the good', still has significance in today's society. Palmer questions whether this is to the same extent that Aristotle cherished these close relationships, but the point remains that distinctions between friendship types are still recognisable.

Throughout the book, Palmer makes no attempt to disguise her admiration of ancient attitudes towards friendship, and reiterates that we have much to learn from antiquity. She extols the value society once placed on cultivating close and enduring bonds with a small tight-knit group of people, and contrasts this with the modern preference for establishing wide networks of what she regards as looser and inferior ties. While Palmer concedes that societies adapt and change over time, she expresses concern that, if people are becoming less willing to invest time in personal relationships, society itself will weaken.

The most compelling sections in *On Friendship* focus on the impact of friendship on children's social and emotional development. Substantial evidence indicates that close or even exclusive friendships can be profoundly beneficial to the development of children's empathy, communication and self-confidence. Perplexing, then, that some schools now actively dissuade pupils from partnering up with a best friend. This is presumably designed to shield youngsters from the inevitable pain that comes when children's notoriously fickle allegiances change or when conflict inevitably arises. Yet, surely, as Palmer demonstrates, there is still tremendous value to be gained from the 'best friend' form of relationship itself, no matter how fleeting. Denying children such relationships can be detrimental to their long-term happiness and wellbeing.

Then again, in a world where 'friend' is increasingly used as a verb, it is argued that children need to thrive in networks of loose ties rather than form deep personal attachments. This may explain schools' growing reluctance to encourage best-friend relationships. Worryingly, some analysts predict that even children who view friendships as disposable are more likely to prosper in the future. Controversial, certainly, and an idea Palmer convincingly refutes throughout the book, armed with ample evidence from educational campaigners, economists and sociologists. This makes *On Friendship* the manifesto society needs for stronger and more satisfying friendships, however we choose to label them.

31 In the first paragraph, what criticism does the reviewer have about the book?

    A It implies that online and in-person friendships are similar.

    B It fails to clarify the distinction between different types of friendship.

    C It ignores the fact that best-friend relationships are unique.

    D It attaches too much importance to people's choice of friendship terms.

32 What do the words 'to this end' refer to in line 15?

    A discussing friendship from an original perspective

    B highlighting the forces that shape modern friendships

    C arguing for friendships to have greater social importance

    D adopting a multidisciplinary approach to the analysis of friendship

33 According to the reviewer, the most striking similarity between modern and ancient relationships is that people have always:

    A categorised and delineated their friendships

    B expected reciprocity in their friendships

    C prioritised close friendships

    D adapted their friendships over time.

34 According to the information in the fourth paragraph, which of the following best describes ancient attitudes to friendship?

    A The value of a friendship may fluctuate.

    B Nurture different types of relationships.

    C True friendships take time to develop.

    D Prioritise quality over quantity in friendships.

35 What point does the reviewer make about childhood friendships?

    A It is impossible to control how children form bonds with people.

    B Children lack the emotional maturity to handle disputes.

    C Preventing children from forming close bonds is counterproductive.

    D Children's friendships are more meaningful than people assume.

36 In the final paragraph, it can be inferred that the reviewer:

    A agrees with school policies on friendships

    B believes that experts are too critical of modern friendships

    C supports the stance Palmer takes on friendship

    D is pessimistic about the future status of friendship in society.

You are going to read four extracts from articles in which academics discuss anthropology. For questions 37–40, choose from the academics A–D. The academics may be selected more than once. Mark your answers on the separate answer sheet.

Anthropology

Academic A

As a field concerned with identifying social practices, cultural anthropology relies heavily on participant observation. Many researchers do this by embedding themselves directly in the target culture. This immersive approach is based on the idea that, by experiencing the culture from within, as part of the community, the anthropologist acquires a richer and more nuanced understanding of customs and social norms. Although there may be value in this methodology in a limited set of circumstances, I remain largely sceptical about the practicability of immersive research. Studying a culture in this way requires substantial personal commitment from the researcher, and is rarely feasible without considerable funding from external bodies. More fundamentally, there is a very real risk that, by integrating so closely into the culture of study, the researcher unwittingly influences subjects' behaviour in some way. This surely compromises the objectivity, and by extension, the integrity of the research.

Academic B

As academics, we are trained to analyse and evaluate information with an impartial eye. I wish we anthropologists could use the same level of objectivity when considering the future of our discipline within the academic landscape. Instead of bemoaning the relative lack of research grants available for our field compared to those given to our colleagues in other disciplines, we have to understand the pragmatic way in which these awarding bodies dish out funding. Investing in anthropology research makes little sense when all the evidence indicates that the subject is in decline. It pains me to say this, but, both in terms of attracting undergraduate enrolments and also retaining students wishing to pursue postgraduate studies, our discipline lags behind comparable subjects such as sociology or even philosophy. We need to make more of a concerted effort to promote anthropology across a variety of channels. Making the subject more accessible to people will surely lead to more public engagement.

Academic C

One of the most pervasive misconceptions about cultural anthropology as a discipline is that it is far less academically rigorous than other research areas. Sadly, those who perpetuate the myth that anthropology isn't a valid academic discipline are causing considerable damage to what is in fact a vital field of study. Anthropology has much to contribute to the world because it investigates the very essence of humanity. Sadly, the amount of financial backing available to academics these days is shrinking, and awarding bodies are forced to make difficult decisions regarding how to allocate their limited funds. I fear that, all too often, anthropologists are unfairly passed over due to a lack of understanding about the importance of their work. It may be contentious, but I'd argue that researchers working in fields perceived to enjoy a greater level of public approval receive a disproportionate amount of financial support from research councils.

Academic D

In recent years, a handful of entertaining anthropology experts have found their way onto the nation's TV screens, bringing the subject to the masses. Of course, anything that generates interest in our field has to be applauded, especially as anecdotal evidence suggests that this is at least partially responsible for the upturn in applications for anthropology degree courses. It's also true that the 'fly-on-the-wall' format of many of these programmes demonstrates the importance of gaining an insider's perspective when conducting anthropological research. However, I have some reservations about how anthropology is portrayed by the media. Popular academics do a fantastic job of bringing their subjects to life. However, most of the anthropology content on TV does little to dispel the popular notion that the subject is 'fluffy' or 'easy'. In their quest to sell anthropology to general audiences, these broadcasters tend to downplay the seriousness of the discipline.

Which academic:

has a different view to Academic D concerning the profile of anthropology in higher education?

| 37 | |

expresses a different opinion to Academic A about immersive research?

| 38 | |

has a similar opinion to Academic B concerning the level of financial support in the field of anthropology?

| 39 | |

has a similar opinion to Academic C about the reputation of anthropology as a subject?

| 40 | |

You are going to read an extract from a magazine. Six paragraphs have been removed. Select from the paragraphs A–G the one that fits each gap (41–46). There is one extra paragraph that you do not need to use.

In Praise of...The Hoover Dam

In the latest in the Modern Marvels *series, Helen Shaw discusses her love of the American dam.*

Forget San Francisco's Golden Gate Bridge or New York's Empire State Building. As impressive as these iconic structures are, when it comes to jaw-dropping American constructions, Nevada's Hoover Dam is in a class all of its own. While I don't actually remember what initially spurred my interest in it, I was certainly enamoured with the Hoover Dam from an early age. In fact, my fascination grew throughout my childhood as I came to learn more about this unbelievable feat of engineering.

41	

In the end, I didn't have an opportunity to make a trip to Nevada until I was in my twenties, but in the intervening years my love of the Hoover Dam had expanded into a more general interest in civil engineering. This meant that, when I finally got to see the Hoover Dam, I appreciated its ingenuity on even more levels, and it far surpassed my already high expectations. I have returned a few times since and each time I am bowled over by its magnificence.

42	

To put these proportions in context, it is worth pointing out that, when it opened in the 1930s, the Hoover Dam was the tallest dam of its kind in the world and, for several years, it was also the world's largest hydroelectric plant. The project was unquestionably ambitious because its purpose was to dam the mighty Colorado River. In doing so, Lake Mead, the largest reservoir in the country was created, and this became a popular leisure attraction for activities such as sailing.

43	

That a project of such magnitude was even contemplated during the Great Depression is important. Following the Wall Street crash of 1929, America entered a severe downturn that lasted throughout the 1930s and beyond. Unemployment was at an all-time high as industrial output plummeted. In light of this, the Federal Government's decision to invest the unprecedented sum of $48.8 million to build a giant dam and hydroelectric facility can be regarded either as a bold move to kickstart the economy, or as a potentially ruinous gamble.

44	

Cities in Nevada had hoped to benefit economically from the sizable influx of labourers. In particular, Las Vegas lobbied to serve as the headquarters of the dam project. However, the Federal Government did not want its landmark project to be associated with a city that it viewed as representative of questionable morality. Instead, a new city, Boulder City, was constructed on the understanding that residents would be subjected to strict social rules, the likes of which were not in place elsewhere in Nevada.

45	

Viewed from this perspective, the Hoover Dam signalled an intention to restore the nation's confidence and to enter a pioneering new phase. Of course, the Hoover Dam is not unique in this sense. Most public works are inevitably a reflection of the core agenda of those in power at the time. Whether it is a commitment to achieving environmental sustainability or economic prosperity, or a desire to address the needs of a particular group in society, large-scale public projects inevitably reveal a lot about a government's priorities and philosophy.

46	

A Yet, the superlatives of the final product only tell part of the dam's story. Even more compelling is how it was constructed in the first place. From the outset, the scale of the undertaking was remarkable, particularly given the socio-economic context of that time.

B Yet another thing I love about the Hoover Dam is its balance between ingenuous functional design and a commitment to aesthetic form. For instance, the inclusion of Native American motifs and tiles, and Art Deco sculptures is simply breath-taking.

C Arguably, the establishment of new residential areas in the surrounding desert landscapes is an example of how, both literally and figuratively, the Hoover Dam shaped more than a body of water. For some, the project is the embodiment of the 'American Dream'.

D Even without these financial implications, any construction project involving a workforce of 5,000 people is something to be admired. Most of these workers were new to the state, raising the question of how they and their families would be accommodated.

E Not that the seven-million tourists visiting the Hoover Dam each year necessarily care about such lofty matters. Nor do visitors need to be as obsessed with engineering as I am to appreciate the beauty of its Art Deco design. A trip there is highly recommended.

F Seeing it in person, it is impossible not to be impressed by its sheer size. The dam itself is 726 feet in height and an impressive 1,244 feet long. The site covers an area of almost 250 square miles, and spans two states.

G In fact, I must have driven my parents to distraction by constantly begging them to take me across the Atlantic so that I could see the Hoover Dam for myself. Trifling matters of distance, airfares or other practical limitations mean very little to children!

You are going to read a magazine article in which five industry experts give their opinions about the future of publishing. For questions 47–56, select the expert (A–E) using the separate answer sheet. The experts may be selected more than once.

Which expert makes the following statement?

The popularity of some digital products may boost sales in other publishing sectors.	47
Financial considerations have a disproportionate impact on smaller companies in the publishing industry.	48
There is growing specialisation within the publishing industry.	49
The publishing industry suffers due to the misconceptions surrounding it.	50
Publishers' products are becoming more affordable for consumers.	51
Relatively few people make purchasing decisions based on personal beliefs.	52
Many consumers no longer want to read books in their entirety.	53
Writers are becoming less reliant on the support of major publishers.	54
Digital formats have yet to encourage new customers to enjoy reading.	55
The publishing industry is sufficiently flexible to keep up with changing trends.	56

A New Chapter?

Is the publishing industry in crisis? Read on to discover what five experts have to say about the future for booksellers and publishers.

Expert A

Publishing is not known for its dynamism. Instead, it seems to be painted as rather a staid industry that rarely innovates. However, we need to be careful not to confuse a sense of heritage with an unwillingness to keep up with the times. Obviously, the publishing industry has existed for such a long time, and maybe that's why people assume it is quite a conservative or traditional industry in which to work. Yet, the irony is that this couldn't be further from the reality. The industry has survived as long as it has by responding to consumers' needs and embracing new trends, as highlighted by its near-wholesale move towards digital publishing. Being saddled with a reputation it doesn't deserve means it has difficulty attracting graduates into the industry, which is a great shame.

Expert B

Much has been made of the growing popularity of eReaders and eBooks read on mobile devices, and there's no doubt that such innovations have transformed the publishing landscape. It has never been easier to self-publish, and this, with an increasing number of small, independent publishers, has meant that established publishing houses are facing unprecedented economic pressures. People's relationship with reading itself has also transformed. The rise of downloadable, bite-sized digests of books speaks volumes, if you'll forgive the pun. Whether it is because of time constraints or other factors, many people now actively seek out these summarised versions, not as a back-up choice but as their new default way of reading. This is particularly the case in non-fiction genres, where people just want to take in chunks of information. This sector is set to explode in the coming years.

Expert C

As a commercial proposition, eBooks and indeed audiobooks are certainly attractive. Digital innovation is helping publishers become more agile and cost-efficient. Even so, there is scant evidence that the newer formats have succeeded in increasing interest in literature amongst reluctant readers. Instead, what they have done is herald a new era of choice for existing readers, and I suspect people are alternating between various formats according to their needs at a particular time. In fact, there are even indications that consumers are motivated to buy print copies after having enjoyed audiobook versions. For this reason, I expect the publishing industry to invest more in this format, for instance by signing up more household names to narrate them. If this happens, perhaps then the joys of literature will finally reach new audiences.

Expert D

Any discussions about the future of the industry have to acknowledge that there is a vast difference between the commercial prospects for mainstream publishing houses with all their financial resources and those of special-interest or niche publishers. For the latter, there are simply not the economies of scale to enable them to invest in the latest technologies or diversify their offerings. That has always been the case to a certain extent, but I fear that the gulf will only widen over time, and some businesses may well be squeezed out of the market by more powerful competitors. Aside from a core of loyal consumers who will always opt to use independent sellers out of principle, I suspect the majority of readers will be more inclined to rely solely on major book retailers and publishers.

Expert E

All companies have to adapt to market forces and consumer trends to survive, and the publishing sector is no exception. The impact of eBooks and audiobooks has made it easier for people to discover new genres and writers with relatively little outlay. Unquestionably, there will always be a place for the large publishers that strive to be all things to all people. However, more and more people are finding their own reading 'tribes' through word-of-mouth recommendations and social media. This, coupled with the rise of online book clubs and websites where readers can get personalised recommendations based on their interests, is generating something of a literary renaissance. This explains the boom in publishers choosing to focus on specific literary genres or to limit themselves to particular types of content.

Answer sheet

Name _____

Date _____

Part 5

Mark the appropriate answer (A, B, C or D).

0	A	B	C ▬	D

31	A	B	C	D
32	A	B	C	D
33	A	B	C	D

34	A	B	C	D
35	A	B	C	D
36	A	B	C	D

Part 6

Add the appropriate answer (A–D).

37	38	39	40

Part 7

Add the appropriate answer (A–G).

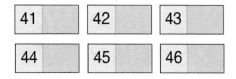

41	42	43
44	45	46

Part 8

Add the appropriate answer (A–E).

47	48	49	50	51
52	53	54	55	56

PROSPERITY EDUCATION
www.prosperityeducation.net

© 2021 Prosperity Education – 'Cambridge C1 Advanced' and 'CAE' are brands belonging to The Chancellor, Masters and Scholars of the University of Cambridge and are not associated with Prosperity Education or its products

Cambridge C1 Advanced
Reading: Parts 5–8

Test 8

You are going to read an article in which the writer discusses fashion design. For questions 31–36, mark the appropriate answer (A, B, C or D) that you think fits best according to the text.

On Fashion

In 1905, the Spanish-American philosopher George Santayana pilloried fashion as producing 'innovation without reason, and imitation without benefit'. Santayana is far from the only intellectual lacking a passion for fashion. While the explosion of university-level fashion design courses has helped to legitimise fashion, both as an outlet for artistic expression and as a subject worthy of academic scholarship, it continues to be viewed with considerable disdain by many public intellectuals. For instance, fashion has yet to enjoy the same elevated status as fine art or architecture. Of course, commercially speaking, fashion design dwarfs these other artforms by a long way. Given this, one is compelled to wonder whether its mainstream appeal has actually hindered rather than helped fashion as an art form claim its rightful place alongside other creative endeavours.

If this is indeed the case, it wouldn't be the first time that an art form has been overlooked due to what is tantamount to intellectual snobbery. Whether it be TV drama, graphic novels or digital photography, cultural commentators have often expressed aversion to art that happens to capture the public's imagination, or at least they have been slow to recognise its creativity. In any case, and no matter how indirectly, the creative concepts found on *haute couture* catwalks eventually filter down and are translated into wearable garments with mass appeal. That this happens should neither negate nor enhance the intrinsic value of fashion design as a form of artistic expression. Fashion design must be judged on its own merits, not simply on its impact on clothing as an industry.

While fashion inevitably influences what is worn around the world, terms such as 'style', 'dress' or 'trends' are not interchangeable synonyms for 'fashion design'. Fashion design is an art form that uses the human body as a canvas, upon which the interaction of textiles, form and colour can be applied to express abstract concepts in much the same way as with other visual arts, like painting or sculpture. Similarly, fashion design may draw its inspiration from a wide range of aesthetic, scientific or social themes, just like any other creative vehicle. Furthermore, a distinction must be made between the act of making political statements via one's sartorial choices and fashion design as a creative outlet for personal expression. For instance, wearing a t-shirt with a political slogan fulfils a communicative rather than an artistic role, one which could just as easily be fulfilled by holding a banner.

What perhaps distinguishes fashion from other art forms is that it is a medium with an end product ultimately intended to be actively used rather than passively received. Hence, fashion is arguably co-constructed by the wearer. People evaluate design elements, such as cut, pattern and colour, and select those that they believe project their ideals and personal values to the world. In this sense, fashion serves as a cultural artefact. This point is underlined by the growing body of research analysing the historical and social significance of fashion design, and the carefully curated items displayed in fashion institutes and museums.

Not that we should look at fashion, or indeed any artform, with a dispassionate eye when it comes to social responsibility. Art should both represent society but also help shape it. What's more, given the universal consumption of fashion, this platform is ideally placed to help set the social agenda. For instance, it is to its credit that fashion has long been associated with the advancement of women in society, both by shedding light on gender inequality and helping to remove gender boundaries. Similarly, fashion can and should be instrumental in highlighting the need for sustainable development. Criticisms of the field for its wasteful approach to natural resources are justified, yet it should also be recognised that fashion is at the vanguard of sustainable design practices. By raising public awareness on important issues in an arguably more accessible manner, fashion takes the lead for other artforms to follow.

Fashion finds itself in a curious position within the arts since it is simultaneously ridiculed for its perceived frivolity while also intellectualised by academics who impose novel interpretations of it. Ultimately, while the medium may not appeal to every commentator, it has a role to play in public discourse, and its artistic credentials cannot be denied, whatever one's personal taste.

31   In the first paragraph, what point does the writer make about the status of fashion design?

    A   Its growing academic profile may have contributed to its economic success.

    B   Its commercial success may have caused it to be taken less seriously as an art form.

    C   It has overtaken other creative subjects, in terms of university enrolments.

    D   It has mainly been viewed as an innovative branch of the arts.

32   In the second paragraph, what does the writer imply about cultural commentators?

    A   They take an elitist stance when judging artistic integrity.

    B   They are enthusiastic about embracing modern forms of art.

    C   They show the same interest in fashion design as they do in digital media.

    D   They pay more attention to high fashion than they do to popular trends.

33   Why does the writer refer to t-shirts with political slogans in the third paragraph?

    A   To argue that fashion is a matter of personal interpretation.

    B   To differentiate between the concepts of form and function.

    C   To highlight the role the human body plays in art.

    D   To draw parallels between artistic expression and political discourse.

34   The writer draws a distinction between fashion and other art forms because fashion:

    A   is directly influenced by societal norms

    B   provides insights into the public's world views

    C   has an interactive relationship with its consumers

    D   attracts consumers from every part of society.

35   In the fifth paragraph, what does the writer say about the relationship between fashion and social justice?

    A   Fashion may be held to higher ethical standards than other art forms.

    B   Fashion should receive more recognition for its contribution to feminism.

    C   Fashion is primarily a mirror that reflects important issues in society.

    D   Fashion has an ambiguous relationship with environmental causes.

36   The overall aim of the text is to discuss:

    A   how the creative medium of fashion design fits into the arts

    B   what fashion represents to society in general

    C   whether fashion has a positive impact on culture

    D   whether criticisms of fashion are justifiable.

You are going to read four extracts from articles in which health experts discuss health and lifestyle. For questions 37–40, choose from the experts A–D. The experts may be selected more than once. Mark your answers on the separate answer sheet.

Wellness
Four experts discuss health and lifestyle

Expert A

The notion that consumers are becoming increasingly well-informed about healthy eating should be qualified with a degree of caution. People's understanding about the importance of achieving a balanced diet and the effects of excessive sugar consumption is certainly better than it used to be. However, while consumers may have taken on board and embraced these key principles, they are also exposed to a wealth of confusing, contradictory or even erroneous information that hampers their best efforts to make wiser nutritional choices. This, rather than consumer indifference, best explains why the nation remains in poor health. One has only to peruse the supermarket shelves to see the issue. In every aisle, products scream about their nutritional credentials and make ambiguous claims of being 'light', 'healthy' or 'natural'. Consumers cannot be reasonably expected to make sensible choices when food manufacturers make misleading or unverifiable claims. Tighter legislation concerning food labelling is surely the key to improving the nation's health.

Expert B

These days, the phrase 'you can't outrun a poor diet' is ubiquitous on wellbeing websites and blogs. Implicit is the suggestion that while people are incorporating exercise into their daily routines, their efforts will yield negligible results because they continue to eat the wrong things. It's certainly a valid point because, when it comes to our overall health, eating well is just as important as staying active. However, the premise that people tend to prioritise working out over eating healthily is flawed. If anything, while there is clear evidence that people are willing to change their eating habits, their lifestyles remain far too sedentary in general. This has to be addressed. The authorities should be commended for what they have achieved so far, in terms of improving nutrition education in schools and establishing useful dietary guidelines, but now similar efforts need to be directed towards encouraging people to exercise more regularly.

Expert C

In recent years, great strides have been made in the quest to improve the nation's health. Inevitably, many of the government-led public health campaigns have thus far centred on improving what I refer to as young people's nutritional literacy. What I mean is that, through initiatives run by the ministries of education and health, this generation of schoolchildren has a solid understanding of the building blocks of a healthy diet. This is certainly to be celebrated, as should the steps taken to promote healthy eating amongst adults. The government is right to focus its efforts on confronting the nation's attitudes to food, because this is crucial to people's health. I predict that in the coming years, public health campaigns will communicate a more holistic message about food. There will be more emphasis on the connection between healthy 'eating in' and improved cognition, sleep and moods.

Expert D

For me, diet and nutrition should remain at the top of the government's public health agenda. There are still far too many people suffering from preventable health conditions as a direct impact of poor nutrition. Of course, it's tempting to assume that ignorance is to blame for this, if only because many consumers rarely cast a critical eye over the nutritional information on food packaging when they shop. However, this misses the point somewhat. Consumers are still relying far too much on convenience- or processed-food items, regardless of whether they opt for the so-called 'healthier' versions of these products. This is, without a doubt, the issue that must be addressed because, in other aspects of lifestyle, progress is being made. After all, many of the people claiming that they have no other alternative but to rely on unhealthy ready-meals manage to find the time and money to go to the gym every day.

Which expert:

has a similar view to Expert B about whether most consumers are committed to making healthier food choices?	**37**
has a similar opinion to Expert C concerning the impact of government intervention on health?	**38**
expresses a different opinion to Expert A about the most effective strategy to improve people's nutritional choices?	**39**
disagrees with the other experts regarding which aspect of people's lifestyle should be targeted to improve public health?	**40**

Shooting Star?

As someone who rarely deviates from default point-and-shoot camera settings, it's fair to say that, at best, my photography skills are rudimentary. Any decent shots I've ever managed to achieve have been as much through luck as by design. No doubt tech-savvy followers of this blog will appreciate that, until recently, many of the snazzy shots therein have benefitted immeasurably from the nifty image filters that you can apply when uploading pictures on this platform. How would someone like me fare on a college digital photography course?

41

Fortunately, the course I applied for seemed to be intended specifically for those not exactly blessed with an overabundance of artistic talent or technical skill. Run by the local college and available to anyone in the local community, the course assumed no prior knowledge of photography. Participants simply required a camera or camera phone to enrol. In fact, the first session involved nothing more taxing than familiarising participants with the most useful camera functions, all while keeping the technical jargon to a minimum.

42

Having a tutor to guide you in person made the learning process far easier, and the course content was tailored to the participants' specific needs. The weekly assignments honed in on specific areas, such as shooting in particular lighting conditions or considering the composition of a shot. This enabled me to develop a more critical eye and fired up my enthusiasm to incorporate more images into my blog. I was developing more confidence to capture people and places, and to share them online.

43

I hadn't expected to cover such topics on a course aimed at complete novices, but, actually, it makes a lot of sense. Never before have people been able to take and share images with such speed and ease. The ubiquity of people snapping away on their phones and instantly uploading the results online might suggest that we are becoming rather thoughtless about what we share and the potential impact this might have on others. These issues were addressed in the course in a thought-provoking but ultimately practical way.

44

Chief among these is, of course, privacy. Even if a photographer's intentions are wholly legitimate, they must consider the subject's feelings, especially if the image will appear in the public domain. It is incumbent on photographers to ensure that they obtain permission before pointing a camera at someone's face. They must also ensure that their photography is as unobtrusive as possible. Ultimately, if someone expresses a desire not to be photographed, the only ethical thing to do is to respect their wishes.

45

Such issues also extend to respecting buildings and the environment. The tutor impressed upon us the idea that hobbyists have to consider these things as much as those who make their living from photography. For instance, when people take pictures when on holiday, it's easy to get carried away instead of respecting the local environment. Photography can disturb wildlife, especially when using flash photography. Similarly, people should not clamber over ancient ruins or fragile rocks in the quest for a perfect shot.

46

A Not that I harboured any particularly creative ambitions with my own photography. My humble aim was simply to gain a basic primer in the core skills needed to improve my photos of scenic landscapes and fast-moving subjects, not to become an award-winning photographer.

B Of course, with so many photo-editing tools readily available, this raises philosophical issues in itself. Can we morally or legally claim ownership of an image if another person has altered it beyond recognition? It's an interesting question, given how frequently images are distributed online.

C And that's before you delve into the legalities of photography in public places. One cannot simply assume that anyone or anything is fair game because different places are subject to different laws. The responsibility lies with the photographer to know the rules.

D I'm also taking my shots in a more mindful way, with greater awareness of and concern for my surroundings and subject. That's because the course has raised my awareness of the ethical issues involved in photography, especially the digital medium.

E Equipped with both practical techniques and a deeper appreciation of photography etiquette, my skills have improved beyond belief. I haven't dispensed with editing tools altogether, but I now use them with far more restraint, and typically to achieve a specific effect rather than to correct my flaws.

F For instance, one subject of discussion concerned photographing people in public places. Many photographers like to capture people going about their daily business in candid moments, rather than setting up highly stylised, posed or staged shots. This raises several interesting ethical questions.

G This was a key selling point for me. Whenever I've consulted online sources to get help with my photography, they were all full of terminology that left me more bamboozled than before. This dented my hope that digital photography skills could be mastered.

You are going to read a magazine article in which five industry experts discuss productivity. For questions 47–56, select the expert (A–E) using the separate answer sheet. The experts may be selected more than once.

Which advisor makes the following statement?

Don't confuse productivity with workload.	47
Having an external form of accountability helps people stay focused.	48
People produce their best work when their work conditions suit them.	49
Work allocation should be tailored to individual needs.	50
One's physical environment has a considerable impact on one's productivity.	51
Well-intentioned advice about time management can be counterproductive.	52
Make strategic decisions about how to maximise limited time.	53
The most effective goals to set are tangible ones.	54
People have a tendency to postpone the most challenging tasks.	55
Most productivity issues are caused by an inability to identify the requirements of a task.	56

Time Management

What are the secrets to being more productive? Here, five experts share their tips and insights.

Expert A

I'm deeply sceptical about the validity of many so-called productivity 'hacks' that purportedly shave hours off a person's working day. This is patently not the case. If it were, such methods would have become standard practice in the workplace. Instead, employees need a degree of autonomy in how they manage their work, by deciding how much time to devote to different tasks and when to prioritise them, based on their personal work rhythms. Of course, many people still benefit from help with planning their projects. Typically, the downfall of people who find it difficult to manage their time is that they have underestimated the challenge level or time involved in completing the various components of their work. This is where managers or colleagues can offer guidance and feedback.

Expert B

The notion of a 'one-size-fits-all' approach to time management is a misconception. Plenty of people find that a high-pressure environment with continual looming deadlines is what they need to spur them on. It brings out the best in them because it focuses their mind. By the same token, others can only thrive in workplaces that encourage decidedly more methodical work rhythms. Whatever a person's preference, the reality is that we often find ourselves faced with seemingly impossible tasks or an overwhelming workload. In these circumstances, it is useful to conceptualise time allocation in budgetary terms. We have a finite number of resources available, so differentiate between the essentials that must be achieved before considering any additional items that can be put off until more time becomes available.

Expert C

Being your own boss comes with its own challenges, most notably having to manage one's time. While the shackles of corporate life may feel restrictive at times, employees often have their daily duties mapped out, enabling them to know exactly what is expected of them. What's more, having to report to other people is often incentive enough to remain on track and avoid distractions. By contrast, when you are left to your own devices, there are far more distractions competing for your attention. Freelancers tend to be more productive if they designate a particular space that they can associate with work. This can be anywhere of their choosing, provided that the area is comfortable, quiet and conducive to work. Noisy or cluttered areas will only serve to distract rather than inspire.

Expert D

It's time to debunk the idea of multi-tasking as a smart way to streamline one's workload and fit more into the day. Multi-tasking may seem like an attractive proposition at first glance, and, undoubtedly, those who advocate it genuinely believe that it can benefit people. Sadly, though, this isn't supported by research. Studies have demonstrated that dividing one's attention across multiple tasks at once is ineffective. The time saving is negligible at best, but as it typically results in all of the tasks being executed poorly, additional time is often required to address mistakes. When it comes to prioritising tasks, start with the most demanding work first. Leaving such things until the end, while a common tactic, is ill-advised. If something requires substantial concentration or thought, tackle it first when you're at your most alert.

Expert E

The adage 'work smart, not hard' crops up in virtually every article about how to improve work productivity, and there's certainly a lot of truth in this advice. The amount of work one does may not have a bearing on whether such labour bears fruits. Likewise, another key distinction is the difference between taking a break to recharge and refocus, and wasting time on activities that distract you from your main purpose. To address this, make other people aware of when you won't be available. This reduces the likelihood that your energies will be diverted elsewhere. You should also make yourself accountable by outlining a clear action plan for each day. This needs to include specific and achievable targets rather than vague ideas that are impossible to quantify or evaluate.

Cambridge C1 Advanced Reading

Answer sheet

Name _____

Date _____

Part 5

Mark the appropriate answer (A, B, C or D).

0	A	B	C	D

31	A	B	C	D
32	A	B	C	D
33	A	B	C	D

34	A	B	C	D
35	A	B	C	D
36	A	B	C	D

Part 6

Add the appropriate answer (A–D).

37	38	39	40

Part 7

Add the appropriate answer (A–G).

41	42	43
44	45	46

Part 8

Add the appropriate answer (A–E).

47	48	49	50	51
52	53	54	55	56

Answer key

Test 1 Part 5		Key words from the questions	Clues from the text
31	C	...first paragraph... / ...cultural significance...can be challenged	...is debatable / ...explore other aspects of popular culture
32	C	In line 13...'their way' / ...linguistic terms	...specialist terminology / ...the expressions...
33	D	...third paragraph...suggest...shipping forecast / ...academic research...limited in scope	...scholars / ...most research...remains focused on the narrow theme....
34	A	...analysing...from an historical perspective / ...incomplete understanding...programme's appeal	most academic work...prioritises the concept of heritage...However, this does not entirely explain why the shipping forecast resonates with as many people as it does.
35	C	...poetry...fifth paragraph.../ ...linguistic structure...powerful effect	...unique sentence patterns and rhythms are...soothing. / ...therapeutic qualities...poetry is the key...calm and gentle rhythm of the bulletins
36	A	main aim of the book / social attitudes to the shipping forecast	...the popularity of the programme / ...this broadcast is held in such high regard / why then does the programme attract global audiences? ...the present books explores alternative interpretations

Test 1 Part 6		Key words from the questions	Clues from the text
37	D	...similar concern to Reviewer A...scope of the book	...makes little attempt to suggest...A missed opportunity...readers...may be left questioning...
38	C	...different opinion from the others / how effectively Anwari defends...	...her arguments are flawed or unconvincing at times,...fails to draw a clear distinction... / Anwari provides compelling evidence for... /...uses a wide variety of examples that successfully demonstrate... / Anwari persuades us...the depth of her research is impressive
39	B	...different opinion to reviewer C...professional credentials affect the content	...Anwari's own links to the business world prevent her from being more objective / ...Anwari once ran a success business...this lends...personal authority to the book
40	D	similar view to reviewer B...is unlike Anwari's other books	...uncharacteristic reluctance...In a departure from the commentary found in her other titles,...

Test 1 Part 7		Clues from the key	Clues from the text
41	F	...display comparable dedication to their mission...guardians of biodiversity and food security...	custodians of the written word...safeguarding of our shared cultural and social history... / This is no minor undertaking
42	A	Viewed from this perspective...more akin to...than that of a cultural organisation...environmental insurance policy	...seeds are primed for future use, should the need arise / ...seems only prudent
43	E	As well as lessening...impact of natural disasters...	...mitigate the harm caused by flooding, droughts or forest fires... / ...others take a more 'productivist' approach
44	G	...scientific innovation is not without criticism...large corporations wielding their power...exacerbate economic disparity	...enabling agri-businesses to develop plant species designed to optimise crop yields / Ethical concerns aside ...

| 45 | C | Another perceived shortcoming...should be banked...not always easy to predict which seed varieties...cannot tolerate the scientific processes | ...efficacy of seed banking has been challenged / ...assuming that seed banks...ascertain which seeds to store...can survive the seed banking process |
| 46 | D | Fortunately,...on-site ways to preserve an even greater variety of species... | preserve species at their source would be a preferable approach |

Test 1 Part 8		Key words from the questions	Clues from the text
47	C	...difficult to identify...aspect of mainstream sport...missing from esports	...hours of training,...coaching...also expected to be in peak physical condition...just like professional athletes...how then does an esports professional differ from an Olympic athlete?
48	D	...participation in esports has no bearing on...other activities	...enjoyment of esports doesn't preclude...from taking up other sports...
49	E	Esports...additional activity to...improve...physical skills	...help athletes enhance...fine motor skills hand-eye coordination...gaming has become a popular activity amongst professional athletes
50	D	team games...skills can be developed via gaming	...acquire skills...ordinarily learn through playing sport with their peers
51	C	Fitness ...must...highest level of esports	Esports professionals...expected to be in peak physical condition
52	B	audiences...unlikely to be impressed...esports	fail to inspire spectators expecting to watch exceptional athletic feats
53	A	substantial demand...broadcasters...esports events	fans' thirst for esports coverage
54	B	gaming community...suffer...integrated into other...events	Olympic Games...wouldn't serve esports well...potentially alienate the existing esports fan base...overshadowed by more popular sports
55	A	...scope for esports...increase in popularity	...no reason why esports can't extend its reach
56	E	controversial content...detrimental...esports' reputation	...games that...glorify violence...esports...image...difficult to market

Test 2 Part 5		Key words from the questions	Clues from the text
31	B	...first paragraph...people's attitudes to leisure. / Discussing leisure habits...pride	tell you all about it... / ...advertising their commitment to their chosen hobby...boast about
32	A	In line 14...'this alone' / ...financial considerations	...prohibitively expensive / ...economic means...
33	D	...third paragraph / ignores...importance of context	Making no concession to cultural relativism...depicts...universal rather than context-specific
34	B	...marathon running / attracts...personality	...character traits... / appeal to people who...determined or goal-oriented
35	A	...fifth paragraph...tribalism./ ...changed...hope to gain	...shift in people's relationship...people now expecting far more than simple enjoyment
36	C	Miriam Carter / focuses too much...academic analysis	...intellectualising the banal has reached its limits

Test 2 Part 6		Key words from the questions	Clues from the text
37	B	...different view to Academic D...impact of companies...protect the environment	...heightened scrutiny may be forcing companies to reconsider their actions...positive steps...are being taken by companies...progress is being made...there are causes for cautious optimism / protecting the environment has unfortunately yet to become a core feature of corporate practice...corporate engagement in environmental issues rarely moves beyond being a supplementary activity
38	D	...different view to Academic A...influence of technology on public attitudes	...ability...connect and share...played a major role in...popularising the subject...online activism has been particularly notable...raising public awareness... / ...social media has facilitated the sharing of information between like-minded individuals...let's not overstate...
39	C	...agrees with Academic D...changes in public perceptions	environmentalism has moved into the mainstream...there has been a genuine shift in society's attitudes to environmental issues / ...public interest in environmental issues has grown
40	A	similar view to Academic C...which stakeholder...has ultimate responsibility	legislation and cooperation between states...the true barometer of society's progress / governments now realise that it falls to them...without this vital step, nothing meaningful can be achieved

Test 2 Part 7		Clues from the key	Clues from the text
41	G	my latest assignment...found myself pondering...should my outfit be...?	open-mindedness...key skills...as a features writer.... / That wasn't the only reservation
42	B	This is the first myth...don't revolve around...laughter...little to distinguish it from other...	...spending an entire day laughing awkwardly... / The point of difference...
43	F	'fake it until you make it'...discernible impact on...performance	... pretending to laugh...create genuine joy in itself / Making it work in practice
44	D	...my initial discomfort...fellow participants...encouraging one another	...embarrassing at first / this sense of teamwork...silly without judgement
45	E	...left feeling relaxed...body ached...lifting weights	...physical effects...effect on muscles
46	A	Being open-minded does indeed pay off.	...if nothing else...far from being a passing fad

Test 2 Part 8		Key words from the questions	Clues from the text
47	C	External influences...organise school timetables	given the increasing governmental scrutiny...reluctant to allocate teaching time
48	A	do not confuse...specialist subject...class activity	drama lessons in the school timetable are kept distinct from...drama activities as...pedagogical tool
49	B	useful...teaching career-based skills	...gain meaningful practical experience...future careers...help medical students
50	D	important...expose students to culture	discovering new worlds...broadening their creative horizons
51	E	educational experts...in favour...teaching drama	...receives widespread support within educational circles

52	**C**	deserves...place...curriculum	Overlooking subjects like drama...misguided...Hopefully, drama...will be reinstated...taught at school
53	**E**	needs to...improve...quality...drama teaching	must be...to the same rigorous standards...taught by specialist teachers with professional training
54	**D**	offered to all pupils, regardless of...talent	innate aptitude...drama has intrinsic value in itself...
55	**A**	drama can enhance...different subjects	teaches...skills that are easily transferable
56	**B**	need...additional study...drama teaching	little research has been conducted...further light should be shone

Test 3 Part 5		Key words from the questions	Clues from the text
31	**A**	...first paragraph...contemporary theories... / less attention...conscious learning	current thinking presents language...rather than...skill to be practised and perfected
32	**C**	In line 15...'doing so' / applying	...applied in real-life contexts...
33	**A**	imply...teaching activities...second paragraph / learners...find them boring	...forced to memorise...endure endless
34	**B**	...third paragraph...distinction between / popularity of language learning...education...society	...language learning is actually...a revival outside formal educational contexts / ...language apps, websites, social media groups...booming
35	**D**	...fourth paragraph...popular stories / ...culture...language	...source of national pride... / ...tales...origins of expressions...enter folklore
36	**C**	...fifth paragraph...language / elastic properties	...language has never been set in stone. / ...language is fluid... / we can re-shape language

Test 3 Part 6		Key words from the questions	Clues from the text
37	**A**	...different opinion to Reviewer D...main aim of documentary	...less a commentary about the relentless rise of social media influencers, and more a critique on the pursuit of fame. / ...the core theme throughout is the extent to which companies now influence these people's online content...
38	**D**	...similar view to Reviewer B...influencers' key abilities	...these influencers rely on marketing strategy and business acumen... / ...spend a lot of time perfecting their SEO rankings and algorithms to identify ways to stay ahead of their rivals...
39	**B**	...different opinion to the others...documentary...realistic	...curious about how authentic the scenes actually were. The parts where influencers complain about all the sacrifices they have to make for their chosen career seemed particularly far-fetched. Whether these scenes were somewhat manipulated for dramatic purposes,.. / In this refreshingly honest documentary, the viewer is shown the reality. / following genuine influencers...real-life documentary... / ...providing a real glimpse into their strange online world
40	**D**	similar opinion to Reviewer C...shortcoming of the documentary	More should have been made of the ethical questions this raises, and this is to the detriment of the documentary. / ...products in question may in fact be...potentially harmful. Why, then, did Andi Fuyako barely cover this issue in *Influencers and Icons*?

Test 3 Part 7		Clues from the key	Clues from the text
41	D	a dislike of pool-based swimming...an increasingly common sight	doing monotonous laps in an over-chlorinated pool...won't necessarily be a pastime that fills you with joy...an entirely different proposition to splashing about in a municipal pool... / current craze for wild swimming
42	A	urban environments...reconnect with nature in the concrete jungle	...it is predominantly city dwellers driving this trend / more general appreciation of the benefits of nature...
43	F	difference between wild swimming and activities based around mindfulness in nature...pushing one's limits	...Likewise, 'forest bathing' is another nature-based practice...involves relaxation techniques / enticing prospect perhaps, but one that is not without its risks
44	C	...energy expenditure involved in keeping warm ...physical benefits	...water temperatures can range from refreshingly cool to ice cold...it is important for the body to acclimatise / This point is surely underlined by the fact that wild swimming has found a following amongst serious athletes
45	G	...physical conditioning options for sporting professionals...Gruelling	... strength or endurance conditioning to supplement their existing regime...The added physical challenges of swimming in nature add dimensions that swimming in a pool cannot replicate / From the relaxing to the taxing, it is clear that outdoor swimming is a pastime that can be enjoyed on many different levels.
46	E	This responsibility doesn't lie solely with swimmers.	...it is also imperative that outdoor swimmers take every effort to respect the environment

Test 3 Part 8		Key words from the questions	Clues from the text
47	D	policy...should not be informed...public opinion	providing it doesn't determine...decisions...public... debate should be encouraged
48	B	most of the work...space programmes...does not receive...recognition...	vital research...main body of work is ignored
49	D	success...difficult to quantify	...projects cannot be evaluated in terms of simple, measurable outcomes
50	D	Too much importance...economic factors...planning	financial stakes...interferes with...puts significant constraints on...science should not be at the mercy of market forces
51	A	Breakthroughs in technology...result...support from...private sector	corporate world...forefront of scientific innovation... technology we rely on would never have been developed...without an economic impetus
52	B	Policy makers...conscious...public opinion...budgetary decisions	governments have to account for...expenditure... incredibly sensitive to claims...wasting money
53	E	benefits...space exploration...long-term	still in its infancy...investors hoping to make immediate profits...advised to consider alternative ventures
54	C	difficult to overlook...environmental damage space exploration creates	actively contribute to environmental problems... unless...reduce their emissions, enthusiasm will decline
55	E	business opportunities...limited by financial considerations	prohibitively high costs...it will gradually become more affordable and therefore a more viable option
56	A	scope for...include both commercial and scientific purposes	no reason why private companies should not invest... International Space Station...scientific endeavour... should take precedence over...commercial enterprises

Test 4 Part 5		Key words from the questions	Clues from the text
31	D	...first paragraph...mainly attracted to antique shops because... / pleasant customer experience	you can browse in peace...knowledgeable staff...help...enjoyable, hassle-free way to spend an afternoon
32	A	...second paragraph...main reason...popularity of antiques nowadays / ecological benefits	people are becoming increasingly conscious of the environmental choices they make as consumers, and are moving away from cheap, disposable products that wreak significant damage on our planet. This, more than anything, explains the current boom in antique sales
33	C	...third paragraph...classification of antiques / antique...surprisingly difficult to define	mysterious business of identifying an antique... fascinating philosophical puzzle...take precedence over the item's age...To complicate matters further
34	D	...implied...nineteenth-century furniture...fourth paragraph / looks strange...modern interiors	...Sadly, as beautiful and well-made as it is, items from this period are simply impractical in modern homes where space can be extremely limited...From a design point of view, incorporating these pieces into a modern home still adds a sense of history, but the overall effect is harmonious rather than jarring
35	B	...'it'...**line 46** / adding...to a business	this is intended to supplement the firm's existing product offerings.
36	A	...aim of the article / promote interest...buying antiques	The quality of antiques has never been in doubt. There is simply no comparison between hand-crafted antique furniture, which was built to last, and flimsy, mass-produced modern equivalents. / However, it is encouraging to see that there has been a surge in sales... / It's heartening to see the sector flourishing...antiques encourage people to consume in a more responsible, low-waste way.

Test 4 Part 6		Key words from the questions	Clues from the text
37	C	...similar opinion to Reviewer D...book's intended audience	...general audiences...understanding of this core demographic...target readers whose interest in the subject may be limited to curiosity about ...leaders, politicians...king... /...those wishing to focus specifically on the people who have shaped our history.
38	A	...different opinion to Reviewer D...main aim of the book	... Black seeks to highlight how our views of history have evolved. Thus, *Learning from History* is a historical overview of historical analysis. /...The book explores the motivations of key historical leaders, and the extent to which their military, political or economic policies were influenced by their psychological states of mind.
39	B	...similar view to Reviewer C...Black's coverage of the topic	...the reader is left with a one-dimensional understanding of historical events. For instance, at no point in the book does Black offer any discussion or analysis of the socio-economic contexts that played such an important role in influencing the course of history. / Frustratingly though,...Had he turned his attention to the fascinating but complex factors which shape historical events, it would have made the book ultimately more satisfying.
40	D	different opinion to the other reviewers...impact of Black's writing	while the opening chapters are mildly diverting, Black's tendency to make sweeping generalisations, coupled with his intimate conversational style, soon irritate. As a result, the book is unlikely to keep readers fully engrossed throughout. / ...fast-paced...Black's lively narrative style...to Black's ability to add intrigue... /

Black's gossipy tone throughout is irresistibly entertaining, too. His portrayal of historical figures almost as if they were characters from a soap opera, ensures that the reader is invested in what happens to these people... / with an approachable lightness that neither alienates nor patronises... unquestionable talent for page-turning writing...

Test 4 Part 7		Clues from the key	Clues from the text
41	D	...not everyone possesses a palate sufficiently sensitive to make it...convey clearly the flavours they're experiencing.	...my true calling is as a professional food taster...could my taste buds make the grade? / This ability to identify and articulate the qualities of a food is called 'sensory acuity'...
42	B	To spoil the fantasy further...inevitable monotony...side effects, including mouth ulcers	...far removed from my childhood dream...In reality,... / begs the question why food development entails such painstaking work
43	F	...pinpointing specific flavour profiles...highly sought after...how would I fare...?	...particular combination of flavours...particular target market / Encouragingly...assures me...route into the profession
44	G	...necessary because...taste buds can become fatigued over time...tasters work on a part-time basis.	...regular training to ensure...sensory acuity hasn't diminished / This policy is one measure that food companies employ...
45	C	Protocols and precautions and apart...product requires a high level of expertise.	...independent panels or groups...avoid spicy food...refrain from wearing strong aftershave... / ...a specialised approach due to the complexity of their flavours...
46	E	...the prestige of this specialist position is attractive.	...regarded as master connoisseurs...astounding product knowledge...travelling the world

Test 4 Part 8		Key words from the questions	Clues from the text
47	B	employers...recruitment decisions...combination of methods	companies may supplement these conventional recruitment methods with alternative ways...
48	C	adapt...documentation...reflect the position	CVs should be customised every time they are submitted. Analyse the core requirements of a particular role and...tailor...accordingly.
49	E	methods...companies use...questionable	Nowadays companies may browse...we might challenge the ethics of this...
50	A	official action...stop unfair employment practices	there is increasing legislation designed to protect people from discrimination.
51	D	fundamental purpose of recruitment...changed...employers	Recruitment is no longer simply about selecting an applicant for a specific role. Nowadays, many corporate employers actually use it instead to discover the pool of talent available, before then determining how they can best utilise the most outstanding individuals in their company
52	C	employers...rely on CVs...decide between comparable applicants	CVs are typically the first thing that companies see... can play a pivotal role in differentiating between similarly qualified candidates
53	A	consider...content...application...objectively	never underestimate the importance of unbiased feedback. Put yourself in the position of a complete stranger...

54	D	regardless of current work...it is worth...raise one's professional profile	Even if they are not actively searching for a new position, professionals should continue to develop their personal brand online
55	B	company's unique environment...way it selects its staff	these methods can also give *you* a more accurate insight into a company's specific ethos and corporate culture.
56	E	be mindful...information...available...public domain	professionals are advised to think twice about what they share online, and who can access it.

Test 5 Part 5		Key words from the questions	Clues from the text
31	D	...first paragraph...media coverage / justifiably negative	...hardly make for relaxing bedtime reading...warning...effects of sleep loss...worrying headlines about society's 'sleep crisis' should not be viewed as media hype
32	B	sleep disorders...second paragraph / portrayed...harmful	...unfathomable that TV producers think it is wise to exploit these disorders...In light of this, the sooner sleep conditions are moved up the healthcare agenda, the better
33	D	third paragraph...expresses uncertainty / why...habits ...changed	Whether it has come about by accident or by design, one key point is at least certain: there has been an indisputable decrease in adults' sleep levels
34	C	...recommended sleep guideline...eight hours a night / safe margin of variation...surprisingly narrow	...this will only vary within an extremely limited range...it is a myth that dropping below or 'getting by' on seven hours is safe.
35	A	attitude...most critical of...fifth paragraph. / ...prioritising sleep...sign of weakness	More harmful yet...boastful claims...the deeply insidious message that successful people simply do not need to bother with such insignificant matters as sleep.
36	B	...overall aim of text / draw attention to	convincing evidence that sleep deprivation is rife and its impacts severe / society's fundamental relationship with sleep deserves a rethink / Ultimately, addressing the root causes of sleep deprivation necessitates a fundamental shift in thinking by individuals and society as a whole

Test 5 Part 6		Key words from the questions	Clues from the text
37	A	...similar view to Academic C...influence of media coverage	All too often, AI is portrayed in films and TV shows as a sinister force posing a threat to humanity...the damage is done by their attention-grabbing headlines /...at the risk of offending sci-fi fans or media outlets, that harmful misconception is largely due to the way in which the subject is treated in public discourse
38	B	...different opinion to the others...machine learning...similar to the way humans process information	...super-intelligent machines able to evaluate, adapt and take decisions without input from humans. As this resembles human thought. / machine learning, which is the foundation of AI, is not the same as human thought or intellect... / ...nor should machine learning be confused with human thought.../ AI lacks the flexibility or adaptability of thought associated with human cognition.

39	D	…similar view to Academic B…distinction…different types of AI	That's certainly the case at present with the so-called narrow AI tools we use for a range of purposes. That said, the prospect of general AI, which is yet to happen of course… / Narrow AI will certainly become further embedded in our daily lives without controversy. By contrast, the prospect of 'general AI' attracts far more debate.
40	B	similar view to Academic D…how humans will play a role…future AI	…a far more pressing concern is whether humans will use general AI responsibly and sensibly. / …we need to ensure that we develop these tools in the right way. If we are careless or, worse, unethical in their application, the consequences could be far-reaching and disastrous.

Test 5 Part 7		Clues from the key	Clues from the text
41	C	Yet that is exactly what I had to do…Deciding to…apply…	…I'm the last person you'd expect to see pitching an idea for a start-up. / When I initially entered, I wasn't really expecting to progress very far…
42	F	…go beyond the basic idea stage. In the first heats,…continue to the final round, which involves presenting their ideas to potential investors.	Stop dreaming and actually do something. / If all that weren't daunting enough, this multi-round format…
43	B	With all this encouragement, *Business Brains*…This truly brings out the best in everyone.	…university provides excellent guidance…continue to consult the mentors after the competition / This collaborative mentality makes sense…
44	G	…getting to that point is far easier said than done, despite all the support on hand…scrutinised from every angle…address any issues that arise during this process	there's a high chance that any participant whose business plan is strong enough to get through the initial elimination rounds will win some form of financial backing / …the purpose of this isn't to undermine students' enthusiasm…
45	A	The other aspect I found incredibly beneficial…exactly what entrepreneurs need to demonstrate when pitching to investors.	The feedback from your *Business Brains* peers and mentors genuinely helps you analyse your idea from fresh perspectives / One such element is 'proof of concept'…
46	D	From this perspective, I thought I had a decent chance of progressing to the final…	This demonstrated that my creations were popular, and that people were willing to pay for them.

Test 5 Part 8		Key words from the questions	Clues from the text
47	B	measures…direct impact…economy	city-centre vehicle bans significantly reduce the number of people entering the city to shop or use the local amenities…obvious effect on the city's commercial opportunities
48	A	punish people…not effective…address traffic congestion	positive incentives are far more likely to lead to desirable outcomes than simply focusing on punitive measures
49	D	environmental benefits…key to…success	the plan will only work if the public supports it. Emphasising the reduction in air pollution is likely to be the best way to achieve this support.
50	C	local authorities…starting to take the problem…seriously	…council will impose considerably harsher fines for any traffic violations…the council is committed to addressing the issue…

51	E	likely...popular with most local people	the vast majority of people around here will embrace the measure...
52	D	positives...outweigh the negatives	Surely, this, combined with safer, more peaceful cities, makes any minor inconvenience to motorists a price worth paying.
53	B	local businesses should be consulted	City-centre businesses and traders...Their voices should be heard on important local issues
54	E	specific limits...cars... difficult to implement	vehicle-quota schemes. This approach is about controlling the total number of vehicles at any given time...a prescribed number of vehicles can enter urban areas on particular days, or at certain times during each day...it seems impractical
55	A	drive...necessity rather than preference	the blame is placed solely on motorists. As far as I'm concerned, the core problem is the lack of viable public transport alternatives. Without these, what are commuters, residents and shoppers supposed to do?
56	C	rarely have a major impact...actual traffic levels	Similar policies...the effect they had on the volume of traffic was negligible. All they do is move the congestion elsewhere

Test 6 Part 5		Key words from the questions	Clues from the text
31	A	...quotation from Aeschylus / seldom...perceived...positive	disapproval of lying is relatively clear-cut. Deception is, as Aeschylus wrote over two thousand years ago, the 'foulest plague of all'...the sentiment still resonates...
32	D	express scepticism about...second paragraph / ...non-verbal clues...reliable indicators...deception	Paralinguistic information is believed to reveal...sure-fire signs of falsehood. However, that...open to debate
33	B	tossing a coin / struggle to detect lies accurately	Studies...revealed success rates within the general population are so low as to be...a random coin toss.
34	D	fourth paragraph...liars are most likely / higher pitch	There is evidence that a high-pitched voice can indeed betray a liar's guilt.
35	B	lie detection methods...fifth paragraph / interviewers...influence...responses	build rapport with their interviewees...eliciting fuller samples to analyse
36	C	final paragraph...the writer's earlier works / personal stances	I strive to cast an objectively scientific eye on the subject, and I hope my loyal readers find the resulting book no less interesting for that.

Test 6 Part 6		Key words from the questions	Clues from the text
37	B	a different opinion to the other reviewers...motives...selecting the cast	...casting of three extremely well-known figures from the world of television...signals his desire to conquer contemporary theatre in his latest play. /...the popularity of these high-profile stars was almost certainly a consideration in Astley's casting /...he overlooked a wealth of established theatre actors in favour of TV performers with a wider public fanbase / ...cast performers primarily known as TV presenters...Astley knew the interest this would generate. In the arts, there's no such thing as bad publicity

38	B	a different opinion to Reviewer D...length of the play	meandering final act...should have been significantly shorter... would have been snappier had it been pruned throughout / what feels like a remarkably short three hours
39	A	a similar view to Reviewer B...popular with critics	Both they and Astley thoroughly deserve the praise heading their way from sceptical reviewers. / plaudits... have eluded him. However, this looks set to change with his latest play
40	B	a similar opinion to Reviewer A...uniqueness of the plot	may have been done before, but rarely with such humour or lightness. / Astley's treatment of the subject is fresh, with an unusual plot

Test 6 Part 7		Clues from the key	Clues from the text
41	E	Far from it. I'm keenly aware of the ethical and environmental problems...I regularly call for more responsible actions	But that doesn't mean I view the travel industry through rose-tinted glasses. / Whether that makes me a hypocrite...to hold the travel industry to account while using my platform to actively promote sustainable forms of tourism...
42	B	action at this macro level...the worst ravages of tourism.	authorities have their part to play by introducing more stringent controls on tourism /...when left unchecked, tourism can certainly wreak havoc
43	D	authorities have several tools at their disposal...strike a suitable balance between welcoming tourism while lessening its negative impact. Instituting fixed limits on the number of visitors	...a dilemma...restrictions so draconian...However, half-hearted measures... / quantitative approach... preventing overcrowding...fewer people in a place
44	C	One such success story is Peru's renowned...	world's most celebrated sites have started to set upper caps on visitor numbers, often with impressive results / ...such restrictions make it imperative for travellers to plan ahead to avoid running the risk of being turned away.
45	G	That may sound harsh...to bar visitors altogether. Such drastic action may be the only chance of saving some areas.	It is precisely this selfish attitude that lies at the heart of the problem... / This has already happened...closing these beaches entirely
46	A	optimism in this particular case because the decision...marine life...	...coral reefs can regenerate...underlines the extent of the problem.

Test 6 Part 8		Key words from the questions	Clues from the text
47	D	...cohesive style elements...feel harmonious.	...tying the overall style...together. This is the key to achieving balance in a space.
48	A	The function of a space should dictate...materials	...consider how you plan to use the room. Delicate fabrics...main hubs of activity...withstand a lot of wear and tear. Opt instead for something sturdier.
49	B	Contemporary...at its peak	we're entering a golden age of interior design
50	C	...design rules...rooted in principles...other fields.	core elements of effective design actually take their cue from established scientific principles...is derived from psychology
51	E	Excessive adherence...rules...spoil the feeling of a room	misguided belief that following a specific framework... In reality, and all too often, it simply results in a sterile room.

52	D	...impact of colours...can be manipulated	...emphasising certain colours in a design or toning them down.
53	E	Successful interior design...considering the end user	...rooms should be designed for the person(s) using them...
54	C	Interior design...gaining more legitimacy	starting to respect the skills involved in interior design, and now recognise that it should be viewed in the same way as other creative fields.
55	B	...becoming more adventurous in....interior design schemes	People are now willing to take a more experimental approach to how they decorate their homes.
56	A	Light should be a core consideration...	...important to build the design of an interior based on the amount of natural light in the space.

Test 7 Part 5		Key words from the questions	Clues from the text
31	D	In the first paragraph...criticism... /...too much importance on...friendship terms	Palmer labours the point, insisting that the decision to use 'pal' as opposed to 'chum'...Curiously, she fails to acknowledge...people who use friendship terms interchangeably...regional factors or...simple stylistic preferences.
32	B	'to this end'...in line 15 / ...forces that shape modern friendships	by asserting how contemporary socio-economic structures are transforming the very nature of our social bonds.
33	A	similarity between modern and ancient relationships... / categorised and delineated	Notably, Palmer highlights how the demarcation of friendships is far from a modern phenomenon...but the point remains that distinctions between friendship types are still recognisable.
34	D	the fourth paragraph...ancient attitudes to friendship / ...quality over quantity	the value society once placed on cultivating close and enduring bonds with a small tight-knit group of people, and contrasts this with the modern preference for establishing wide networks...
35	C	...childhood friendships / Preventing...close bonds is counterproductive	Denying children such relationships can be detrimental to their long-term happiness and wellbeing.
36	C	the final paragraph...inferred... / supports the stance Palmer...on friendship	Palmer convincingly refutes..., armed with ample evidence...the manifesto society needs...

Test 7 Part 6		Key words from the questions	Clues from the text
37	B	...different view to Academic D...profile of anthropology...higher education	when all the evidence indicates that the subject is in decline...in terms of attracting undergraduate enrolments, and also retaining students...our discipline lags behind comparable subjects... /...the upturn in applications for anthropology degree courses
38	D	...different opinion to Academic A...immersive research	'fly-on-the-wall' format of many of these programmes demonstrates the importance of gaining an insider's perspective when conducting anthropological research. / ...the researcher unwittingly influences subjects' behaviour...This surely compromises the objectivity, and...the integrity of the research

| 39 | C | ...similar opinion to Academic B...level of financial support...anthropology | allocate their limited funds. I fear that all too often, anthropologists are unfairly passed over... / ...we anthropologists...relative lack of research grants available for our field... |
| 40 | D | similar opinion to Academic C...reputation of anthropology | However, most of the anthropology content on TV...popular notion that the subject is 'fluffy' or 'easy'. / ...pervasive misconceptions about cultural anthropology... it is far less academically rigorous than other research areas. |

Test 7 Part 7		Clues from the key	Clues from the text
41	G	I must have driven my parents to distraction by constantly begging them...see the Hoover Dam for myself.	enamoured with the Hoover Dam from an early age...my fascination with it grew throughout my childhood / I didn't have an opportunity to make a trip to Nevada until I was in my twenties
42	F	Seeing it in person, it is impossible not to be impressed by its sheer size...726 feet in height...1,244 feet long...covers an area of almost 250 square miles	I have returned a few times since and each time I am bowled over / To put these proportions in context...
43	A	the superlatives of the final product...the scale of the undertaking ...given the socio-economic context	the tallest dam of its kind in the world...and the world's largest hydroelectric plant...the largest reservoir in the country... / Great Depression is...a severe downturn...Unemployment was at an all-time high as industrial output plummeted.
44	D	Even without these financial implications... workers...they and their families would be accommodated.	unprecedented sum of $48.8 million to build a giant dam and hydroelectric facility...a potentially ruinous gamble / Cities in Nevada had hoped to benefit economically from the sizable influx of labourers.
45	C	the establishment of new residential areas... the embodiment of the 'American Dream'	a new city, Boulder City, was constructed... / to enter a pioneering new phase.
46	E	such lofty matters	large-scale public projects inevitably reveal a lot about a government's priorities and philosophy.

Test 7 Part 8		Key words from the questions	Clues from the text
47	C	...digital products may boost sales in other publishing sectors	consumers are motivated to buy print copies after having enjoyed audiobook versions.
48	D	Financial considerations...disproportionate impact on smaller companies	a vast difference between the commercial prospects for mainstream publishing houses with all their financial resources and those of special-interest or niche publishers. For the latter, there are simply not the economies of scale to enable them to invest in the latest technologies or diversify their offerings.
49	E	...growing specialisation within the publishing industry	boom in publishers choosing to focus on specific literary genres or to limit themselves to particular types of content.
50	A	The publishing industry suffers due to the misconceptions	Being saddled with a reputation it doesn't deserve means it has difficulty attracting graduates into the industry...
51	E	...products are becoming more affordable for consumers.	easier for people to discover new genres and writers with relatively little outlay.

52	**D**	Relatively few...purchasing decisions...personal beliefs.	Aside from a core of loyal consumers who will always opt to use independent sellers out of principle...the majority...
53	**B**	Many consumers no longer want...books in their entirety.	now actively seek out these summarised versions, not as a back-up choice but as their default way of reading.
54	**B**	Writers are becoming less reliant on...publishers.	It has never been easier to self-publish...
55	**C**	Digital formats have yet to encourage new customers	...scant evidence that the newer formats have succeeded in increasing interest in literature amongst reluctant readers.
56	**A**	The publishing industry is sufficiently flexible to keep up...trends	...has survived as long as it has by responding to consumers' needs and embracing new trends

Test 8 Part 5		Key words from the questions	Clues from the text
31	**B**	first paragraph...status of fashion design / commercial success...taken less seriously	its mainstream appeal has actually hindered rather than helped fashion as an art form claim its rightful place alongside other creative endeavours.
32	**A**	second paragraph...cultural commentators / elitist stance...judging artistic integrity	intellectual snobbery...cultural commentators have often expressed aversion to art that happens to capture the public's imagination...should neither negate nor enhance the intrinsic value of fashion design as a form of artistic expression.
33	**B**	t-shirts with political slogans...third paragraph / differentiate...form...function	a distinction must be made between the act of making political statements via one's sartorial choices and fashion design as a creative outlet of personal expression...fulfils a communicative rather than an artistic role, one which could just as easily be fulfilled by holding a banner.
34	**C**	distinction...fashion and other art forms / interactive relationship...consumer	distinguishes fashion from other art forms is that it is a medium... ultimately intended to be actively used rather than passively received. Hence, fashion is arguably co-constructed by the wearer.
35	**D**	fifth paragraph...relationship between fashion and social justice. / ...ambiguous relationship...environmental issues	Criticisms of the field for its wasteful approach to natural resources are justified, yet it should also be recognised that fashion is at the vanguard of sustainable design practices.
36	**A**	overall aim of text /fashion...fits into the arts	its rightful place alongside other creative endeavours / ...should neither negate nor enhance the intrinsic value of fashion design as a form of artistic expression. Fashion design must be judged on its own merits... / Fashion design is an art form...fashion design may draw its inspiration from a wide range of aesthetic, scientific or social themes, just like any other creative vehicle / fashion serves as a cultural artefact. / its artistic credentials cannot be denied

Test 8 Part 6		Key words from the questions	Clues from the text
37	**A**	similar view to Expert B...consumers are committed...healthier food choices	consumers may have taken on board and embraced these key principles...hampers their best efforts...This, rather than consumer indifference... / there is clear

			evidence that people are willing to change their eating habits...
38	B	similar opinion to Expert C...impact of government intervention	The authorities should be commended for what they have achieved so far, in terms of improving nutrition education in schools and establishing useful dietary guidelines... /...through initiatives run by the ministries of education and health, this generation of schoolchildren has a solid understanding of the building blocks of a healthy diet. This is certainly to be celebrated...
39	D	different opinion to Expert A...most effective strategy...people's nutritional choices	Consumers are still relying far too much on convenience- or processed-food items...This is, without a doubt, the issue that must be addressed. / Tighter legislation concerning food labelling is surely the key to improving the nation's health.
40	B	disagrees with the other experts...which aspect of people's lifestyle should be targeted	their lifestyles remain far too sedentary in general. This has to be addressed / erroneous information...nutritional choices...best explains why the nation remains in poor health / The government is right to focus its efforts on confronting the nation's attitudes to food / There are still far too many people suffering from preventable health conditions as a direct impact of poor nutrition.

Test 8 Part 7	Clues from the key	Clues from the text
41 A	Not that I harboured any particularly creative ambitions...gain a basic primer	How would someone like me fare on a college digital photography course? / be intended specifically for those not exactly blessed with an overabundance of artistic talent or technical skill
42 G	This was a key selling point for me...full of terminology...more bamboozled than before. This dented my hope	keeping the technical jargon to a minimum. / tutor to guide you in person made the learning process far easier
43 D	taking my shots in a more mindful way...course has raised my awareness of the ethical issues...the digital medium.	incorporate more images into my blog...to capture people and places, and to share them online. / cover such topics...
44 F	For instance, one subject of discussion concerned photographing people in public places...This raises several interesting ethical questions.	These issues were addressed in the course in a thought-provoking but ultimately practical way… / Chief among these is, of course, privacy.
45 C	And that's before you delve into the legalities of photography in public places...The responsibility lies with the photographer to know the rules.	if someone expresses a desire not to be photographed, the only ethical thing to do is to respect their wishes. / Such issues also extend to respecting buildings and the environment.
46 E	...both practical techniques and a deeper appreciation of photography etiquette	Similarly, people should not clamber over ancient ruins or fragile rocks in the quest for a perfect shot.

Test 8 Part 8	Key words from the questions	Clues from the text
47 E	Don't confuse productivity...workload	The amount of work one does may not have a bearing on whether such labour bears fruits.
48 C	external...accountability helps...stay focused	What's more, having to report to other people is often incentive enough to remain on track and avoid distractions.
49 B	produce...best work when...work conditions suit	It brings out the best in them because it focuses their mind. By the same token, others can only thrive...

50	A	Work allocation...tailored to individual needs	employees need a degree of autonomy in how they manage their work, by deciding how much time to devote to different tasks and when to prioritise them, based on their personal work rhythms
51	C	physical environment...considerable impact	be more productive if...designate a particular space that...associate with work.
52	D	advice about time management...counterproductive	Undoubtedly, those who advocate it genuinely believe that it can benefit people. Sadly, though...is ineffective.
53	B	strategic decisions...maximise limited time	seemingly impossible tasks or an overwhelming workload. In these circumstances, it is useful to conceptualise time allocation in budgetary terms.
54	E	most effective goals...tangible	specific and achievable targets rather than vague ideas that are impossible to quantify or evaluate
55	D	tendency to postpone...challenging tasks	most demanding work...Leaving such things until the end, while a common tactic...
56	A	issues...caused by...inability to identify the requirements of a task.	Typically, the downfall of people who find it difficult to manage their time is that they have underestimated the challenge level or time involved in completing the various components of their work.

Made in United States
North Haven, CT
05 May 2022

18897960R00057